Second edition
Copyright © 2010 Alastair Sawday Publishing Co. Ltd
Published in November 2010 by Alastair Sawday Publishing

Alastair Sawday Publishing Co. Ltd,
The Old Farmyard, Yanley Lane,
Long Ashton, Bristol BS41 9LR, UK
Tel: +44 (0)1275 395430   www.sawdays.co.uk

ISBN-13: 978-1-906136-44-4

Series editor: Alastair Sawday
Editorial Director: Annie Shillito
Editor: Jackie King
Editorial Assistance: Carmen Cox
Writing: Jo Boissevain, Ann Cooke-Yarborough, Nicola Crosse,
Monica Guy, Jackie King, Helen Pickles
Production: Julia Richardson, Tom Germain
Maps: Maidenhead Cartographic Services
Printing: Butler Tanner & Dennis Ltd, Frome, UK
Cover design: Walker Jansseune
Cover photograph: Mark Bolton

Photography

Mark Bolton

Wooda Farm
Agaric Rooms at Tudor House
North Wheddon Farm
Binham Grange
Abbey Home Farm
Allt-y-bela
Gliffaes Hotel

Lesley Chalmers

Manor Farm
Daffodil & Daisy
Southlands Farm
The Kinmel Arms
Neuadd Lwyd

Rob Cousins

Primrose Valley Hotel
Cornish Tipi Holidays
Hornacott
Fingals
Beara Farmhouse
Royal Oak Inn
Church Cottage
Harptree Court
The Griffin Inn
Dadmans
Strattons
24 Fox Hill
Ty-Mynydd
The Peren
Little Quebb Cottages
Old Country Farm
Annie's Cabin
Timberstone Bed & Breakfast
Gallon House
Thistleyhaugh
West Coates
Court Farm
The Yat

Lucy Pope

The Bull Hotel
Huntstile Organic Farm
Barwick Farm House
1 Leicester Meadows
The Victoria
fforest

Go Slow
England & Wales

Alastair Sawday

Foreword by
Kate Humble

Special places to stay (with page numbers)

Contents

Foreword by Kate Humble

Some time ago I was in a bookshop looking for nothing in particular, when my eye caught sight of a book called 'Go Slow England'. It was a guide to places, communities and people who have immersed themselves and live in tune with their surroundings. It was an invitation to pause, to look, to smell, to experience some of England's simple and uncomplicated pleasures. If we took our foot off the accelerator, if we let ourselves be led by our senses rather than by our watches, we could experience this lovely country in an entirely new way. The birthday was coming up of a friend who, like so many of us, worked too hard and made life convenient and possible by resorting to microwave, takeaway, sofa and re-runs of 'Friends'. I bought the book and gave it to him. A month later he left his job. Maybe that book had something to do with it...

The book was published by Alastair Sawday. I have long been a devotee of Alastair Sawday's guide books. His 'special places to stay' really are exactly that: places that have a distinct personality of their own, that make guests feel they have been terribly clever to discover them. I have a deep-rooted loathing for the corporate, for the impersonal, for those warren-like hotel corridors with no natural light that make your heart plummet. No such corridor would make it into his Special Places to Stay. What sets them apart is the fact that the people running them – often the owners themselves – seem to garner as much enjoyment from sharing their place, the food from their gardens, their home cooking, as we, their guests, get from being there. By chance, it seems, I had stumbled on just some of the joys of the Slow movement.

The Slow movement is all about taking time to appreciate food, landscapes, buildings, chance encounters. By supporting the slow movement we are supporting a way of life that I believe has true benefits for people, for communities and for our countryside. It is a celebration of the traditional, of the old-fashioned, of a gentler pace of life and I know I won't be the only person who yearns for all those things in the heat and horror of an inhuman rush hour in a city centre.

I am lucky enough now to be able to call Wales my home. It is a truly special part of the country and one to pass through slowly and savour. I had one criticism of 'Go Slow England' – it didn't include Wales. Now it does.

Introduction by Alastair Sawday

The more I write about Slow the more I learn how vast and many-sided a movement it is. It is a simple way of articulating deep human wisdom. Countless proverbs, such as 'Covetousness is the father of many unsatisfied desires', and 'Provision in season makes a rich house' touch upon Slow. Whenever we are enjoined to be thoughtful, thrifty, generous, meditative, appreciative of small things, rooted to place and nature – we are being encouraged to be Slow.

Of course there is more. The Slow Food movement, begun in Italy by a radical food writer called Carlo Petrini, has taken on political overtones to match its tireless crusade for good honest food and production methods that respect place and people. Wherever a fine old variety of fruit, cheese, bread, wheat, rice – and so on – is threatened, the Slow movement comes to the rescue. In part this is an instinctive clinging to old certainties, in part a profound awareness of their value and of the dangers posed by their replacements. The grubbing up of an old orchard of apple trees, or the loss of the last bakery in an ancient village – these are real threats to what makes us civilised and happy.

I once spent some happy days with the Amish of Michigan, and learned something about the wisdom of Slow. Always bear this in mind; very little is necessary for living a happy life.

Marcus Aurelius speaks for the Amish, who have cleverly decided that the way to survive the challenges of modern life is to pick and mix. When they perceive that a piece of technology is useful but dangerous, they are wary of it. Thus, a telephone can disrupt families and social ties, but

is useful. So they keep them outside their houses and use them only at certain hours. The internal combustion engine has shattered the peace, enabled children to go far away and wastes time and money on a Herculean scale; but it has great strength. So the Amish put the engine on the platform of a horse-pulled cart and use it to drive, say, the rotating blades of the harvester. The horses are useful and economical, and provide work. The engine gets the job done quickly. Jobs and time are both saved, a rare trick. The Amish

seem to be Slow naturally, though whether they have as much fun as the rest of us – I don't know.

Forgoing vacuous indulgence is part of the essence of Slow, but there are replacements a'plenty: conviviality, the pleasures of eating fine and honest food, the nourishment of good relationships. What is more, and far more important, is the stark fact that unless Mankind forgoes much of his material excess then future generations are doomed to pay a terrible price. We are living way beyond our means.

Fast living is nothing short of morally bankrupt. Neither does it bring satisfaction. Michael Crichton perceptively wrote: "In other centuries human beings wanted to be saved, or educated, improved or freed. But now they want to be entertained. The great fear is...of boredom." How sad is that? The inability to find meaning in simple things lies at the heart of this boredom.

So, Slow is a rediscovery of 'meaning', of beauty too. The Special Places we have chosen to feature in this beautiful book are all owned by seekers after meaning and beauty, many of whom have left behind the thrusting chaos of urban life (though I confess that I love my life in urban Bristol) for the quieter countryside and its "dappled things – its skies of couple-colour as a brinded cow; for rose-moles all in stipple upon trout that swim; fresh-firecoal chestnut-calls, finches wings; landscape plotted and pieced..." as tenderly evoked by Gerard Manley Hopkins. A childlike delight in life and its wonders seems to follow years of Slow living. Cynicism stands in the way of contentment.

I am frequently asked how I can write about Slow while encouraging you to travel. After a sharp intake of guilt, I explain that Man has always travelled – but never so quickly. Why should I not encourage some slowing down and reveal pleasures that might otherwise pass us by?

Better, might I not introduce you to others, who can lead by example where I cannot, who can show you new things, teach you new skills?

There is the young lad who is nurturing bees in the middle of London and creating some of the country's best and most pure (no fertilisers in London gardens) honey. I should mention, too, Alex James – the ex rock-star from Blur who gave up a life of excess to tend a farm in Oxfordshire and now creates cheeses. That's a fast-to-slow journey and he, like so many, discovered that it is the simplest things that bring most happiness.

In this book you will, too, read of Richard Cooper who owns The Bull Hotel in Bridport. He was in the music industry also but has, with his wife, created a pub/hotel that helps to knit the community together. "Local groups hold meetings here, artists display their work, the Literary Festival is sponsored by The Bull and local builders, architects and furniture makers have all played their part in the look," says Richard. "We all work together and play cricket together. We're here for the long haul.

"You will also discover The Yat in mid-Wales – rambling and ancient and with its roots in the fourteenth century. Once the squire's house, it was part of the Cwm Mawr estate and the most important house in the Glascwm hamlet. It was once on the drovers' route and the landscapes described in Dylan Thomas's hymn to his nature-bound childhood at his uncle's farm seem untouched. The owner, Krystyna (top left), shares Thomas's love of nature and paints pictures not with words but oils.

Hilary Chester-Master of Abbey Home Farm near Cirencester is proudest of creating the Soil Association apprenticeship scheme. "A hundred years ago there were twenty work horses here and a stable boy's day was 5am to 7pm. That's now unthinkable but this country sorely lacks skilled growers and you can't learn the job in a classroom. So I and a couple of others pushed and pulled, hassled and argued, and got the idea accepted. Apprentices stay for two years and work in the garden in exchange for board, lodging, the minimum wage and a lot of

mentoring. There are also a number of formal training modules. They are all so eager to learn, we love having them. Our first apprentice has just started a box scheme in Ireland! I feel it's a triumph."

I salute all these fine people however, as I write, I am painfully conscious that I am as far from being Slow as I can be. Yet for the moment I am revelling in the writing of this introduction, enjoying my daily bike rides to the office, the mornings drinking coffee with colleagues by the harbourside, the views from the garden over to the Somerset hills, the company of neighbours on our shared terrace,

the ease with which we can get into the countryside from our Bristol house. Perhaps one can be slow in a city, too?

My wife, Em, grows flowers in her pots on the terrace and vegetables in her allotment, teaches yoga and meditates every day. She is contentedly Slow, and is well able to tolerate the occasional dash to somewhere else. However, we spend too long at our computers, consulting our diaries and don't read enough. Cherished friends are seen all too rarely. There is perhaps no room for complacency after all.

Alastair Sawday

Cornwall   Devon   Dorset

Somerset   Sussex   Kent

ENGLAND: SOUTH

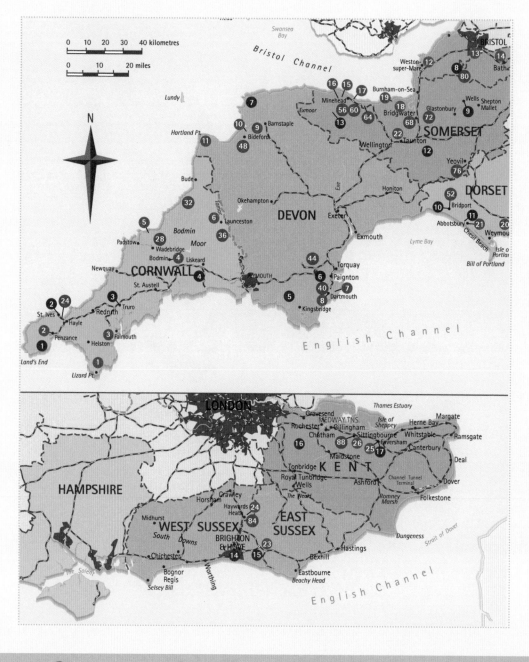

Slow travel

1. Minack Theatre
2. Train from Penzance to St Ives
3. Potager Garden
4. Bodmin & Wenford Steam Railway
5. Port Quin Kayaking & Coasteering Tours
6. Cowslip Workshops
7. Coleton Fishacre
8. Paignton & Dartmouth Steam Railway

9. Tarka Trail Cycle Track
10. Tapeley Park Gardens
11. Lavender Farm
12. Brean Down
13. The Observatory
14. Bath Boating Station
15. Selworthy Village
16. Burrowhayes Farm Stables
17. Dunster Castle

18. Coleridge Cottage
19. Kilve Beach
20. Hardy's Cottage
21. Abbotsbury Gardens
22. Hestercombe Gardens
23. Boating on the Ouse
24. Bushcraft
25. Saxon Shore Way
26. Doddington Place Gardens

Slow food

1. Cove Cottage Tea Garden
2. Porthminster Café
3. Lemon Street Market
4. Cornish Orchards
5. The Oyster Shack
6. Riverford Field Kitchen

7. Mortehoe Shellfish
8. New Manor Farm Shop
9. Wells Farmers' Market
10. Washingpool Farm Shop
11. Hive Beach Café
12. Julian Temperley

13. Dunkery Vineyard
14. Bill's Produce Store
15. Breaky Bottom Vineyard
16. The Hop Shop
17. Shepherd Neame

Special places to stay (with page numbers)

24. Primrose Valley Hotel
28. Cornish Tipi Holidays
32. Wooda Farm
36. Hornacott
40. Fingals
44. Agaric Rooms at Tudor House

48. Beara Farmhouse
52. The Bull Hotel
56. North Wheddon Farm
60. Royal Oak Inn
64. Binham Grange
68. Huntstile Organic Farm

72. Church Cottage
76. Barwick Farm House
80. Harptree Court
84. The Griffin Inn
88. Dadmans

Slow travel

1 Minack Theatre
Porthcurno (01736 810471)
Spectacular cliffside, open-air theatre whose first performance – 'The Tempest' in the summer of 1932 – was lit by batteries and car headlamps. Explore by day, see a play at dusk. www.minack.com

2 Train from Penzance to St Ives
Passing the huge sand dunes of Hayle Towans and the sweep of Carbis Bay you avoid the parking madness of sweet St Ives. Buy a day ticket and hop on and off as you like, on one of the most scenic branch lines in the UK.

3 Potager Garden
Constantine (01326 341258)
Stroll through this former garden nursery on a summer weekend – for flowers, vegetables, fruit trees and a lush tangle. Glass canopied veggie café & foraging courses... read Dan's blog.
www.potagergardennursery.co.uk

4 Bodmin & Wenford Steam Railway
Bodmin (0845 1259678)
A thirteen-mile round trip that takes in a viaduct and Bodmin Moor. From the station at Bodmin you can walk to Lanhydrock House (01208 265950) for a touch of 'Upstairs Downstairs' and spectacular magnolias.
www.bodminandwenfordrailway.co.uk

5 Port Quin Kayaking & Coasteering Tours
Port Quin & Port Gaverne (01208 880280)
Join in a three-hour kayak tour: soak up the views and the wildlife, drop a mackerel line over the side, kayak surf at low tide.
www.cornishcoastadventures.co

6 Cowslip Workshops
Launceston (01566 772654)
Courses on quilting, knitting, vintage textiles and, for children, 'Keepsake Fairies'. Fabric shop, tea and coffee too.
www.cowslipworkshops.co.uk

7 Coleton Fishacre
Kingswear (01803 752466)
Arts and Crafts house, designed in 1925 for the d'Oyly Carte family, with exotic gardens that plunge down the valley to the coastal path. Fab cream teas, great views.
www.nationaltrustorg.uk

8 Paignton & Dartmouth Steam Railway
Paignton (01803 555872)
Chug along the Torbay coast to the Dart estuary, hop on the ferry at Kingswear to lovely Dartmouth, then puff back again. Round trips also include river cruises.
www.paignton-steamrailway.co.uk

9 Tarka Trail Cycle Track
Braunton (Cycle Hire: 01271 813339)
Head along the estuary, named after Henry Williamson's otter, to Fremington Quay Café (organic ciders, cream teas).

10 Tapeley Park Gardens
Bideford (01271 860897)
Crumbling splendour: a lovers' evergreen tunnel and lily-dotted lake. Tea and cakes in the old dairy and occasional 'Health and Harmony' weekends. www.tapeleypark.com

11 Lavender Farm
Cheristow (01237 440101)
Come to swoon over Eric's 120 varieties of lavender, farmed under a countryside stewardship scheme. Gifts and a tea room.
www.cheristow.co.uk

12 Brean Down
Reached via 211 steps from the beach, this blustery National Trust peninsula is home to peregrines, kestrels and a bramble smothered temple. Picnic on the springy turf in the shelter of a hollow and take in stupendous views. Bring jumpers, dogs and toddlers on reins.

13 The Observatory
Bristol (0117 9241379)
The only 'camera obscura' open to the public in England, housed in an 18th-century windmill on a green Clifton hill overlooking Brunel's iconic bridge.
www.about-bristol.co.uk

14 Bath Boating Station
Forester Rd, Bathwick (01225 312900)
Victorian boating station almost in the centre of Bath. Punts (dodgy), skiffs (romantic), can be hired by the hour or the day. Find a nettle-free bank, bring the sun hats and hamper.
www.bathboating.co.uk

15 Selworthy Village
Thatched model village on Exmoor's Holnicote Estate, that climbs the hill to a 15th-century church with gorgeous views to Dunkery Beacon, the highest hill in Somerset and the South West. Trot back down for a reviving tea in the National Trust cottage.
www.nationaltrust.org.uk

16 Burrowhayes Farm Stables
West Luccombe
(01643 862463)
Escorted rides for all ages in the Horner Valley and on the moors. One of the few stables left on Exmoor.
www.burrowhayes.co.uk

17 Dunster Castle
Dunster (01643 821314)
Subtropical gardens, historic, thriving village and magnificent 17th-century castle whose plasterwork ceilings are vacuumed only every fourth year to protect them.
www.nationaltrustorg.uk

18 Coleridge Cottage
Nether Stowey
(01278 732662)
Home of Coleridge, who lived here from 1797 to 1800. The village is lovely and has a farm shop and tea room/bistro. The Coleridge Way marches you across the Quantock Hills, Bredon Hills and Exmoor – all the way to Porlock.

19 Kilve Beach
At low tide, a favourite haunt of geologists with spectacular rock formations and fossils. To the east, in the 15th-century remains of a chantry, is a pretty tea garden open all year.

20 Hardy's Cottage
Higher Bockhampton
(01297 561900)
Birthplace of Thomas Hardy who wrote 'Far From the Madding Crowd' here. Small delightful cob and thatch cottage sparsely and authentically furnished, with pretty cottage garden.
www.nationaltrust.org.uk

21 Abbotsbury Gardens
Abbotsbury (01305 871387)
Superb 18th-century walled coastal garden leading to a gentle combe with camellias and magnolias in woodland, specimen trees and rare plants. Drop down to Chesil Beach with your hammer and chisel and dig out a fossil.
www.abbotsbury-tourism.co.uk

22 Hestercombe Gardens
Cheddon Fitzpaine, Taunton
(01823 413923)
Acres and acres of gardens, from Georgian landscaped parkland to Arts & Crafts intimacy, designed by Lutyens and planted by Gertrude Jekyll.
www.hestercombe.com

23 Boating on the Ouse
Barcombe (01273 400414)
The Anchor Inn has boating rights over a gorgeous stretch of river, down to the weir at Sutton Hall. Set aside two hours for a paddle upstream and back – plus hamper.
www.anchorinnandboating.co.uk

24 Bushcraft
Nutley (01444 482619)
Hone your survival skills, from friction firelighting and making shelters to snaring and cooking game. "Serious but fun" courses for adults and families last one to four days.
www.wildwoodbushcraft.com

25 Saxon Shore Way
On the long-distance footpath leading to the white cliffs of Dover is a flat, wildlife-rich stretch (four nature reserves): Conver Creek, Harty Ferry, the village of Oare, Faversham.
www.faversham.org

23 Doddington Place Gardens
Sittingbourne (01795 886101)
Spectacular rhododendrons and azaleas Easter to end June – plus Edwardian rock garden, herbaceous borders, fine trees, clipped yews, lunches and teas.
www.doddingtonplacegardens.co.uk

Slow food

1 Cove Cottage Tea Garden
St Loy (01736 810010)
On the Smugglers Path between Porthcurno and Lamorna, a magical spot overlooking gardens that spill down to the sea. Clotted cream teas: tea from a local plantation, cream from the Lizard.

2 Porthminster Café
St Ives (01736 795352)
Linger over fresh oysters, bouillabaisse, local mackerel - worth every penny. Overlooking St Ives Bay.
www.porthimnstercafe.co.uk

3 Lemon Street Market
Truro (01872 273031)
Cornwall's sole city, Truro, is a foodie hub. Visit the covered market for smoothies and chutneys and fairtrade goods. Farmers' market Wed and Sat.

4 Cornish Orchards
Westnorth Manor Farm, Duloe (01503 269007)
Take your pick from juices, ciders and punches.
www.cornishorchards.co.uk

5 The Oyster Shack
Stakes Hill, nr. Bigbury (01548 843558)
Under tarpaulins and disused sails, simple, local produce and fresh fish. Bring your own wine.
www.oystershack.co.uk

6 Riverford Field Kitchen
Buckfastleigh (01803 762074)
Plonk yourself down at a communal table for a memorable organic meal (preceded by a tractor-trailer tour, or a walk at your own pace). Popular, must book.
Closed November-March.
www.riverford.co.uk

7 Mortehoe Shellfish
Mortehoe (01271 870633)
Stop for a perfect crab sandwich after a coastal walk from Lee to Mortehoe, or an evening lobster platter.

8 New Manor Farm Shop
North Widcombe (01761 220067)
Tuck into the cakes and meals in the Stable Tea Room before exploring this wonderful farm shop.

9 Wells Farmers' Market
Market Place. Wednesdays, 9am-2.30. In lovely Wells, smallest city in England.

10 Washingpool Farm Shop
North Allington (01308 425424)
North Devon beef cattle, Jacob cross sheep, veg and soft fruit at this family-run farm: fresh, tasty and traceable. Restaurant too.
www.washingpool.co.uk

11 Hive Beach Café
Burton Bradstock (01308 897 070)
Big tented café on Chesil Beach: sustainable salmon and line-caught bass chalked up on the boards as rollers beat on the shore. Cosy on a winter's morn, a haven on sunny days.

12 Julian Temperley
Kingsbury Episcopi, Martock (01460 240782)
One hundred varieties of cider apple fermented and distilled with passion "and a certain amount of roguery". An exceedingly fine cider brandy, too.
www.ciderbrandy.co.uk

13 Dunkery Vineyard
nr Wootton Courtenay (01643 841505)
Whites, reds and bubbly, produced from seven gorgeous acres on Exmoor.
www.english-wine.com

14 Bill's Produce Store
Brighton (01273 692894)
Fresh food utopia and vibrant place to meet and eat. Dried peppers decorate ex-bus depot rafters and film-set puddings are to die for. There's nothing like it - except for its sister store in Lewes.
www.billsproducestore.co.uk

15 Breaky Bottom Vineyard
Rodmell (01273 476427)
Great sparkling wines from, perhaps, the most beautiful vineyard in the country. "Sussex is the new Champagne."
www.breakybottom.co.uk

16 The Hop Shop
Shoreham (01959 523219)
Pick your own apples, treat yourself to lovely Chelsea Gold-winning hop bines and dried lavender, essential oils and traceable farm foods. Special.
www.hopshop.co.uk

17 Shepherd Neame
Faversham (01795 542016)
Britain's oldest brewer. Gaze into the mash tuns, learn how Spitfire and Bishop's Finger are made. Tutored tastings.
www.shepherdneame.co.uk

Pubs & inns

Star Inn

St Just, Cornwall
Close to Land's End, "the last proper pub in Cornwall", an 18th-century gem. Pub games thrive in the low beamed, spic and span bar, and coals glow on wild nights. There's mulled wine in winter, live music and a great family room. 01736 788767

King's Head

Ruan High Lanes, Cornwall
In a village with a church and a creek, a small pub with a big heart. Pine stools, a comfy old sofa, quirky touches, a real fire, and gleaming tables for tasty meals of crab pâté and Cornish sirloin. All in Roseland countryside. 01872 501263

Bridge Inn

Topsham, Devon
A must for ale connoisseurs, and for all who love a pub furnished in the old style. High-back settles and a simple hatch inside, a garden by the steep river bank outside, pies, home-cooked hams and Devon cheeses. 01392 873862

Pig's Nose

East Prawle, Devon
Lanes with high hedges weave down to the edge of the world. It's big inside, filled with character and quirky ephemera. A pint, a pie and a paper at lunch and singalongs at night - it's quite something. 01548 511209

Square & Compass

Worth Matravers, Dorset
Splendid old pub with a rare narrow drinking corridor and two hatches, for farmhouse cider and homemade pasties. Live music and cribbage, a winter fire and a sunny front terrace. A popular stop for coastal path walkers. 01929 439229

Lord Poulett

Hinton St George, Somerset
A ravishing inn, French at heart and quietly groovy. Take refuge in the daily papers on the sofa, play boules in the garden, look forward to brilliant barbecues and Sunday roasts. A welcome to all, dogs included. 01460 73149

Castle Inn

Bradford-on-Avon, Wiltshire
Lovely planked rooms - one large, two small - in muted colours, stone walls, real fires and big scrubbed tables. Friendly staff serve great renditions of British pub classics. In historic Bradford-on-Avon, one of the best. 01225 865657

Hollist Arms

Lodsworth, Sussex
Prop up the long narrow bar with a pint of King's Horsham Best, tuck into lamb shank and local-farm potato chips, relax at a table spilled with magazines and games. Pink walls, cheerful chatter, much charm. 01798 861310

Red Lion

Stodmarsh, Kent
In an enchanting village, a 15th-century inn with tiny rooms. Bare boards, log fires, candles on tables, hens in the garden and a very bossy cat. Super-local and delicious food arrives on huge painted plates. 01227 721339

Primrose Valley Hotel

CORNWALL

St Ives has for many years seduced the best-intentioned outsiders, including St Ia, around whose chapel houses began to cluster in the sixth century. The artistic focus of the town has always been remarkable, generating a special buzz. Whistler and Sickert came here in the nineteenth century, setting the tone for a twentieth-century artistic invasion: Ben Nicholson, Barbara Hepworth and Bernard Leach among many others. In 1993 the Tate Gallery opened a new branch here – a giant artistic enterprise.

Today it is not only artists who nurture an affection for the gaily painted and clustered houses of the old part of town, and St Ives's rare sense of isolation. It is far from the main roads and just on the edge of a strange and beautiful part of England around a village called Zennor. There's a very fine pub there, the Tinner's Arms, built for the masons who built the church. It has lovely garden and a fire inside for winter. And if you have a spare two days, the Coastal Path will carry you beyond to Land's End, along cliffs and land's edges as dramatically lovely as any.

Andrew and Sue were seduced by the same light that had seduced Whistler. "One crisp April morning we strolled down to Porthminster Café and on into town. It was simply stunning. We had to come and live here." Having persuaded Sue's parents to join them they

bought a tired seaside hotel. Sue was six months pregnant and next door was a building site. They couldn't do much at first but did get rid of the plastic flowers.

"We want to be a positive force in St Ives." Andrew's words are music to our ears, a reminder that tourism can be more than it has largely become; so much of it involves little more than the open-cast mining of local resources and people. Andrew and Sue's determination to make a difference to their community as well as to the environment is an inspiration. They have been wonderfully clever with the limited spaces, creating a house that feels cool, contemporary and calm. It is delightfully fresh and unstuffy, with modern prints, pale wooden floors, bold wallpapers. No two bedrooms look the same, some have views of the bay, and the suite, with its red leather sofa, slipper bath and curved walls, is almost extravagant. Where there were once swirly carpets there is open-mindedness and elegance; where there were just two there are now "nine great staff, the vast majority full-time". They know, too, that they cannot sit still while the town changes around them, which is why they opened their small but perfect REN Room for bio-active beauty and skincare therapies.

From the white wooden balconies you gaze upon the wide

sea. Not the 'sloe-black, slow black, crow black, fishing-boat bobbing sea' of Dylan Thomas, for most of the St Ives sea is kindly and more sparkling blue than black. You feel sheltered from both the sea and the outside world.

Cornwall may well become the first county in England wholly to embrace the new environmental mood. The hotel has built up an impressive list of Cornish food suppliers, cheeses, charcuterie and smoked fish are always available, and drinks from big-brand names – Schweppes, Coca Cola – are eschewed in favour of those from small ones. Hidden from view are other commitments: eco-friendly cleaning materials, a green energy supplier and an emphasis on recycling.

"We don't agree with guests having to be involved in the mechanics of recycling, though," says Sue, "and the last thing we want is to have notices everywhere dictating what they must and must not do. Our staff do all the sorting and our hope is simply that guests will absorb our approach throughout the hotel and take something of our ethos home."

Their sense of community has seen the blossoming of a fund-raising initiative for the Marine Conservation Society. Andrew says, "Five years ago we made a slightly brave move – we added £1 per room per night for the MCS, with an option to have it removed. Over £13,000 has been raised and paid to the Society – all for very little effort."

It has been said that it's not easy being green and Andrew and Sue tussle daily with dilemmas. They want to use eco-friendly everything but the guest still wants to see snow white and fluffy towels. "Grey towels aren't 'in' yet," jokes Andrew, so they continue to allow hot washes. Their door signs

> "Drinks from big brand names are eschewed in favour of those from small ones"

are made from recycled foamex and are printed in Cornwall – consequently they cost around £15 each, which doesn't appear to be a good business decision. "But just as guests have come to expect the best mattresses, bedding and bathrooms, they increasingly expect excellent food and they want to know its provenance. That delights us.

"We hope that guests will appreciate what we are doing and not mind paying a little extra where we simply have to pass on the cost. We want to compete on quality and eco-friendliness, not on price."

So you will find beautiful REN products in the bathrooms, natural products in the REN therapy room and breakfast sausages of a rare deliciousness.

Another nice touch is the £5 discount per night offered to anyone who arrives without a car. St Ives, of course, is a perfect place for such gestures: you don't need a car. Walking can be all you do – along the coastal path in both directions, carrying a picnic made up for you by the staff at the hotel. Or take a bus to Penzance and stop off at St Michael's Mount, thirty minutes away; it is iconic, fascinating and less touristy than its French equivalent. With luck you will walk across the causeway and return to the mainland by boat at a higher tide – or vice-versa. You leave with a sense of having shaken off this century.

Back in St Ives there is so much to do that these journeys may not appeal at all. The town is inevitably busy in summer, but gets more interesting by the year. There is now a Jazz Club, year round, on Tuesday nights, adding another touch to the cosmopolitan mood of a renewed St Ives.

The gradual process of shedding stress can start way before you arrive. The mainline train journey down to Cornwall is one of the loveliest in Britain. You then slip out of St Erth on the branch line and into St Ives station, moments away from the hotel.

"We have a reputation for being eco-friendly and we are determined to do better and better. It's not always easy," says Andrew, "and the dilemmas keep coming. It's only once you set off down the Slow road that you realise what a very long road it is."

Andrew & Sue Biss

Primrose Valley Hotel,
Primrose Valley, St Ives TR26 2ED
- 10 rooms. £100-£235.
- Platters available all year.
- 01736 794939
- www.primroseonline.co.uk
- Train station: St Ives

Cornish Tipi Holidays

CORNWALL

"Sleeping in a tipi is like sleeping in a living organic thing. The smell of the canvas and the twine, the gentle creek of the pole as it sways in the breeze – it's like sleeping on a boat."

The moment you arrive here there's a shift. No computer, no washing machine, no reception, perhaps no car. Family dynamics change, everyone mucks in and, as the rhythm of outdoor life washes over you, somehow there's more time for fun. Lizzie's children are the ninth generation in the family to be born in this parish, and she delights in seeing children enjoying the wildlife and space of sixteen safe acres in a wooded Cornish valley. "Some people barely leave the site – they don't need to if their children are happy making dens in the woods and exploring with new friends."

Lizzie's father farmed the old-fashioned way. "It was slower, less fraught. It didn't destroy the land and the livestock were treated in a humane way."

Lizzie's sister now carries on the tradition. The land was quarried for fifty years and so is untouched by agri-chemicals. Indigo-blue dragonflies hover over lakes and ponds, butterflies flap through buttercups, spotted woodpeckers flit among the woods and tawny owls puncture the night's silence with their hooting.

After time away from her native Cornwall – university then journalism and PR in London – Lizzie came back to have her first child at thirty. "I didn't want to raise a family in London and there didn't seem much point in settling for life as a commuter."

Having made the decision to carve out a greener lifestyle and create the camp back on the family farm, they were surprised by resistance to their plans from some residents and planners. Now most are convinced they are a force for good, although there has certainly been a discrepancy in the lack of official support for their plans given Cornwall's eager promotion of itself in the sustainable tourism arena.

"We continue to explain that a tipi pole doesn't even break the surface of the earth, and that we are facilitating carbon-free holidays. We're also about to build an eco barn with space for washing, drying and storage with a living turf roof, straw bale walls and a wind generator." The greatest irony is that the camp has been deemed ineligible for a Green Tourism Business Award simply because it has always been green. "I was told that as there was no evidence of 'consistent change and radical improvements' – ie. because we have always been green – we don't count!"

Lizzie sourced her American Indian-style tipis made of unbleached canvas from craftsmen in Cornwall, Devon and Wales so there are no air miles and few road miles. Other campsites have since imitated her style and are awash with tipis, yurts and bell tents.

A stay here can be as sociable as you like: in the 'village field', or tucked away in the clearings. Everyone tends to congregate around the firepit under starlit, midnight blue skies; wine and stories are shared, children and grown-ups find new friends.

The tipis are scattered with patterned rugs, gas lanterns create a warm glow, the old camping stove keeps things toasty. Experienced campers know to bring from home the things that make the holiday more comfortable – padded rollmats, woolly jumpers, favourite bedding (pillows recommended).

There are showers as an alternative to jumping in the lake, and flushing loos instead of a trip to the bushes, but this still feels like getting back to basics. The lake is perfect for cooling dips, rowing and trout fishing; there's a stream for toddlers and a warden on site all year round.

Being unprepared for observing nature at close quarters is a mistake. Lizzie tells tales of guests complaining about an influx of slugs and frogs one damp summer, and of being upset by wasps one hot one. "One guest was upset because a dormouse had retreated to her tipi for warmth, snuggled up in her very expensive cashmere sweater and nibbled a little hole."

But those who are not natural campers and who could afford to be in a waterfront cottage in nearby Rock still come, and they come because they want to feel something new, something real. Now you can marry here, too. This magical valley, with its trees and its birdsong, its camp fires, its night skies and its new wood pavilion by a trickling stream is the ultimate place for a Slow wedding.

Fathers have bonding holidays with their sons, groups of friends come to relax and know the children are being safely adventurous, and couples come to simply be – together. There's the Camel Trail to be cycled, the Coastal Path to be walked, the beaches to be discovered (Polzeath for surfers, Daymer for small children) and pretty Port Isaac ten minutes away, where you can buy fish fresh off the boats.

A coracle builder at Falmouth College is keen to run courses on the water. Lizzie has plans for community and education work and is excited about the rise of the eco wedding – especially the stir created by the recently formed Cornish Tipi Weddings.

The vagaries of nature can make or break your experience here – if the sun is shining the experience can't be beat – but you play your part, too. "Some people fall apart in bad weather, others determine to make the most of being here. A plumber and his family stayed last year – he had been declared bankrupt, lost his business and they hadn't had a holiday for four years. They arrived to torrential rain yet each day he and his four children and wife togged up and walked and swam and cooked. He even took it upon himself to keep everyone's spirits high, and inspired us all."

Elizabeth Tom

Cornish Tipi Holidays,
Tregeare, Pendoggett,
St Kew PL30 3LW
- 39 tipis, 1 yurt. From £410-£615 p.w. Short breaks from £230.
- 01208 880781
- www.cornishtipiholidays.co.uk
- Train station: Bodmin Parkway

Extra pictures: Emma Bradshaw, Sandra Lane, Kim Appleby

Wooda Farm

CORNWALL

Buzzards swooping through open skies, honeysuckle twirling amid ancient hedgerows besieged by dancing butterflies, high cliffs splashing into Atlantic waves. When Max dived out of his small London pad into a patchwork of soft meadows, farmland and trees two miles from Cornwall's north coast it was the sense of space that enthralled him most. After fifteen years as an actor and countertenor singer in London's theatres he yearned for an empty space of his own, a space which he could use and share.

Certainly, Wooda Farm is a stage to spark the imagination: tucked into a dramatic cut in the hillside, a rugged backdrop of rocky cliff and towering trees showcases an ancient farmhouse, cottage, stone barn and timber-framed studio strung along a narrow farm track. The land rises in steep tiers, from a stream and spring carpet of bluebells up, up, up past terraced organic vegetable beds to high pastures where Wooda sheep strut. Below the house, tall beech, oak and ash trees wave gently to the rhythm of an Atlantic wind which, up above, buffets the highest meadow and sends a small generator wind turbine into overdrive. And more often than not, the place echoes with the music, talk and laughter of visiting groups in the beautiful stone barn.

It was the barn, semi-ruined but replete with possibilities, that spurred Max to buy the farmstead eleven years ago. Yet even he is genuinely surprised at its success: stone walls rebuilt with local rock and slate, one side yawning with light-gulping swathes of glass, an ingenious counterweighted mezzanine which transforms into contoured auditorium seating. It has won two Royal Institute of British Architects (RIBA) awards and the sincere praise of singers, composers, writers and artists, as well as yoga groups and wedding couples. Says Max: "It's beautiful – much more sophisticated than the simple whitewashed barn I had in mind – but what's important is the space and versatility. You can create anything in a space like this. We want people to make it their own."

Next door, a glass-walled studio teeters on timber tiptoes over the steep valley, wearing a grassy turf hat which slopes naturally down from the meadow above. Hired by artists, writers and musicians, it is designed to blend in with the landscape, allowing inspiration to flood in and the imagination to expand and explore. Max and Gary, along with Max's mother, artist Elspeth Owen, offer a Wooda Arts Award, in which a committed artist wins six weeks' use of the studio – just one part of a plan to make this hidden spot a centre for creative discovery and development.

One suspects it was all preordained. At a recent primary

school reunion, one of Max's teachers brought him his old school project on endangered species. "Even as a child I was into 'saving the animals' and nature conservation," says Max. Nevertheless, breaking with London's bright lights was no simple matter. "It was a bit of a gamble," he admits. "But I was so excited, I felt I was opening up after the claustrophobia of London and regaining some control over my life. And I fell in love with this space – so steep, so wild, so replete with animals and biodiversity. I thought 'Don't just dream about it, do it.' And now? Yes, I'm happy. I feel I have a more rooted existence."

Wooda has grown slowly, organically, naturally. Soon after Max settled in he busied himself: converting the twenty-acre farm to Soil Association-certified organic status, planning the conversion of

> "The studio is just one part of a plan to make this hidden spot a centre for creative discovery and development"

the barn and studio, learning to tend to the animals, twenty-four sheep - each with its own name - a mule 'Morgan' and cob 'Cal', and a flutter of Maran and Black Rock hens. Always a part of Max's vision was that as much food as possible would be grown and made at Wooda. How lucky then that four years into the project he met Gary, an inspired self-taught cook, who soon became intrinsic to his own existence and that of the farm. As Gary, too, slowly divested a previous life, as a specialist NHS nurse, together they cultivated, struggled, learnt and blossomed anew. Max reflects: "I guess when you're doing what's right for you, you attract the right people."

It has proven easy to attract the 'right' people for Wooda, for that includes anyone who relishes nature, creativity, conviviality. Groups using the barn can book bedrooms in the 1600s farmhouse, and everyone gathers by a huge log fire in the flagstone-floored kitchen while Gary cooks, chats, laughs.

Meals, around a communal table, are fresh, seasonal and bursting with flavour: their own tender lamb; home-grown vegetables and salads; mushrooms, hazelnuts, herbs and wild garlic gathered on foraging expeditions; mackerel plucked straight from the sea.

Holiday-makers also have the chance to stay at Wooda next door, in a self-catering cottage only slightly less ancient than the farmhouse. Couples and families hole up here to enjoy the animals and nature, popping to the beach for a swim or a breezy beer at the pub, walking the coastal path, learning to surf, and taking trips to the Eden Project, Tintagel Castle (of King Arthur fame) and the Tate St Ives.

Max and Gary relish the buzz which comes with groups and guests and then disperses. "We're not precious: this isn't a hotel. Don't be surprised by the odd scuff mark, or if we have to dash off to rescue a sheep stuck in a fence. We like to connect with people but leave them free to do their own thing." Sometimes they escape onto the cliffs to watch the sun set over the Atlantic. "The ocean view is so vast – the next stop is Newfoundland."

There is limited space here to describe all that goes on at Wooda Farm. But if you wish to experience warm hosting by an engaging, talented couple deeply committed to their farm and nature; to stay or work in beautiful simple, ancient buildings in stunning, wild landscape; to savour home-grown delicious, organic food, eaten convivially; to enjoy a shared space of immense freedom and creativity... then take note, for Wooda is all these things and more. A place, and people, we applaud.

Max Burrows & Gary Whitbread

Wooda Farm,
Crackington Haven, Bude, EX23 0LF
- Self-catering cottage £295-£625 p.w.
- All inclusive food, accommodation and use of barn space £180 p.p./£230 p.p. for 2/3 nights.
- 01840 230129
- www.woodafarm.co.uk
- Train station: Bude (bus link)

Hornacott

CORNWALL

You are on the cusp of two counties – walk one way up the lane for views of Dartmoor and the other for views of Bodmin Moor, the closer of the two. This is a little-known part of Cornwall, an area through which people pass on their way to the rest of the county. And at the bottom of the steep lane that runs past the house is one of the oldest bridges in Cornwall, Trekelland Bridge on the Inny.

Mining in the Tamar Valley started in the thirteenth century and ruins of mines and mine stacks are bleak witness to the mineral wealth once found in the valley. Three large mines produced copper, lead, tin, tungsten and arsenic. Now the valley is an Area of Outstanding Natural Beauty, with a rich wildlife and a beauty of its own.

Before modern wheeled transport arrived the river was, of course, the main highway. The stone to build the great Cotehele House, a stupendous National Trust manor house overlooking the Tamar, came up the river by boat and was unloaded at Cotehele's little quay.

The Tamar valley was also famous for its fruit; now a few Tamar cherry trees blossom in spring where once there were thousands. Other fruit has fared a little better: apples, pears, strawberries, plums.

Mary-Anne and Jos met in London and lived by Barnes Common for four years. "London is great fun for a young single person, I wouldn't have missed it for the world. But the trip to work got to us, and a certain dissatisfaction crept into our lives. There, a lot of people just talked about schools and house extensions. Down here nobody cares whether you have a huge estate or a tiny cottage. Nobody gives a darn what car you drive, though a Lamborghini might get laughed at. A beaten up old Landrover has far more cachet.

"We had a friend who had bought an old place down here, knowing no-one. We came to stay. After the third or fourth visit, we were heading back to London and we both went very quiet. Then we said, almost in unison, 'What on earth are we doing in London?'"

They moved in 1994, with a family of Jack Russells, in search of a house that would, somehow, earn its own living. Doing B&B did not occur to them until they had moved in. They replaced the roof on the B&B section, once a grain store, and put skylights in. The office below had been a cow byre, with a beautiful, if unappreciated, view.

"We just got on with it. If we had thought about it we wouldn't have done it. We started doing B&B in 1996, giving guests plenty

of their own space. They come into the main house for breakfast, which is a good way to meet up with us.

"We had a few friends when we moved down. Local people can be quite hard to get to know; it just takes time. But the neighbours would leave a bag of vegetables and I would bake them a fruitcake," says Mary-Anne. "Locals fear that people like us are bound to bring change. But Jos was brought up in Devon (his Dad was in the marines) and I had relatives here too, and we have no desire to change anything.

"Someone in London said to me, 'I'd like to downshift when I'm older, too.' The funny thing is, we haven't downshifted: we never sit still. We are far busier than in we would be in a nine-to-five job. Here you use every bit of your body to do something... cutting grass is physically exhausting! And having visitors is fun. They come to explore the Tamar Valley, Cothele House, the gardens, the art. People often stay and come back. They love what they find.

"On a quiet summer's evening, when you can sit out with a glass of wine – can you put a price on that? And there is some poor chap busting his guts in the city and earning a million – is he happy? Not if the chap next door is earning a million and a half!"

Hornacott's claim to be Slow derives from the pace of life, the gradual learning about country ways, the enthusiasm for shopping carefully and for buying real, locally produced food.

"I shop in Launceston. There is a wonderful butcher there who puts out big blackboards declaring which farm each bit of meat came from.

"Kind hearts, soft beds and great sausages!"

I heard something quite astounding one day: a customer picked up a chicken and the butcher said 'it's free range.' To which she replied, 'oh, I'm not having that, you don't know where it has been!'"

Mary-Anne and Jos have an efficient boiler running on oil, and get their water from their own spring. Any attempt to be green is aided by North Cornwall's positive attitude to recycling: clothes, glass, bottles from the door, all with colour-coded bags.

The only barrier to a slow life is the rabbit population. They compete for every vegetable – and tend to win. It can seem impossible to outwit them.

Jos's peaceful office is in the renovated cow byre. He has a kitchen design business, Templederry Designs. "I decided from the start that I wanted to create kitchens that fitted with people's lifestyles, rather than simply supplying a series of boxes that fit a space. It is very satisfying work."

Above his office is the guest suite, equally peaceful, wonderfully airy, nicely self-contained, its lofty sitting room leading into a cool, blue bedroom with twin beds and a spotless little bathroom. You can sit as the sun goes down, admire the changing light and linger over the valley views.

A doorway leads, more prosaically, to an extra little twin, just in case there are more than two of you, and then to the main part of the house for an enthusiastic welcome from the Jack Russells and a generous breakfast at the big dining table. "Kind hearts, soft beds and great sausages!" wrote a visitor about Hornacott.

To a backdrop of grand old trees, the garden, loved and tended by Mary-Anne, tumbles down the slopes over one and a half acres, with sunny lawns and shady spots and seats poised to catch the evening sun. A stream runs through after heavy rain and trickles quietly by in the summer months, its banks aglow with water-loving plants. A collection of old-fashioned English David Austin roses has been introduced. It is a supremely peaceful setting. At the very bottom of the garden is their own hideaway, a Finnish barbecue hut.

"We don't have a lot of time to relax," says Mary-Anne "but we are so glad not to be office-bound. We are happy here."

Jos & Mary-Anne Otway-Ruthven

Hornacott,
South Petherwin, Launceston, PL15 7LH
- 1 twin-bedded suite, 1 twin. From £80. Singles £50.
- Dinner £20. BYO.
- 01566 782461
- www.hornacott.co.uk
- Train station: Plymouth

Fingals

DEVON

Perhaps the essence of Fingal's slow approach is treating every good moment like a fine wine – to be tasted, talked about, then consumed. It would be surprising to find other people running a hotel the way Richard and Sheila do, with a sense of fun and a rare informality.

"In some hotels I have been to you are given table Number 4 when you arrive and there you are stuck – on table Number 4 – for breakfast and dinner," says Richard. "You have the same napkins, talk to no-one and end up whispering to your partner over meals in a peculiarly English way. At Fingals everyone cross-fertilises and joins in. We positively want people to use the place as a social melting pot. It works brilliantly – hardly ever does it go wrong. If people want to eat on their own that is fine; there are two dining rooms and no kids at the big table. The result is something like an informal club."

Some people are uncomfortable with all this, of course – unhappy about the informality, the touches of chaos, the quirky décor. That's what happens if you dare to be different. But for many people Fingals is a home-from-home and they return like swallows, year after year.

"I was in London, burning out, running a restaurant (called Fingals, after my dog) for three years. I was an energetic amateur having a lot of fun, broke all the rules and was successful. One day I got out of bed

and just froze and said to myself. 'I have to get out of here'.

"I had seen a little black and white photo of this building and drove by, but thought 'no way'. I looked at lots of little hotels in Devon and Cornwall but didn't really like the feel they had. To be honest, I don't really like hotels with rules and regulations like breakfast between eight and nine and coming down for dinner at seven."

But Richard did come back and took a look around and thought, what a mess!

"It had been stripped of every ounce of character. Four flats, lino on the floor, shower in the corner of the room, that sort of thing. I had to strip it out and start again. I had one bedroom when I started in 1981, and the hotel renovations are still going on now. It is a labour of love."

Every year the urge overtakes him to build something new. One year it's a barn, the next a folly or an eco cabin. This year it's an extension to the pool. And over the years much of the work Richard has done himself.

He is a driven man, pumping with restless energy. But, compared to his life in London, this is slow – and, of course, provides opportunities for others to wind down. "I didn't come in here with all guns blazing, a big building plan and an architect in tow. It has been done bit by bit and grows organically. It has grown with

personality and with an ethos – and it has taken twenty-nine years."

Fingals is undeniably beautiful, a handsome stone manor house in a tight little valley a mile or so from the Dart. It is dusted with art of all sorts, sculpture and painting by friends – in the garden and in all the rooms. The place bubbles with a mix of serenity and amused vitality. The Folly, a two-storey hut on the banks of the stream, shown in the main picture, is a touch of delightful eccentricity.

Ducks quack across the lawn in the evening pursued by Sheila urging them to bed and getting in the way of tennis (ducks and Sheila both). Dogs roam everywhere; some of them belong to guests. Children run about the lovely garden playing tennis or ping-pong, or having a swim. Adults can be seen quietly reading behind a bush, on a near-hidden terrace or a private balcony. The evening is a time for conviviality, for drinks together in the tiny bar, for laughter and conversation that is rarely dull – for Richard and Sheila are often there enjoying it all. Sheila is a gem: sweet-natured, gentle, fun, patient and generous. She is the spirit in the machine, the cog that turns. Without her Richard would probably disappear into some Quixotic project never to emerge.

The place is far greener than most. "I came down from London with all the eco books and found that running a hotel calls for a hundred compromises. But we are up for it now. We heat the hotel water with solar panels and heat pumps (with a back-up boiler) and the new stream 'eco' room has heavy hemp insulation, a solar thermal mass wall and solar panels for the hot water, which extends to the pool buildings. We buy organic and local food, know our suppliers well and are wide open to new ideas. Walking is a big thing here; just step out of the door and Devon is yours: the Dart, the sea, the woods and miles and miles of green lanes. A little further is Dartmoor."

Fingals is not for the fastidious. The occasional spider may be overlooked; the bedrooms are an eclectic mix. Some are huge and open-plan, such as the green-oak barn where a whole family can stay and can self-cater. Others are smaller and simpler, even a touch traditional. All have antique beds, Vi-Spring

mattresses and their own bathrooms. Dinner is served in the wood-panelled dining room at one long table (or in a separate dining room if you prefer intimacy). It is a mellow, lovely space that encourages conversation. The food is fresh, French and delicious.

The generosity of Fingals reaches far. Richard often takes guests out on his old wooden speedboat, or on a launch. He is game for anything – showing you the Dart, lending you a bike and even pedalling with you – with his own brand of energy. Above all, he and Sheila really do want you to do your own thing. Come down to breakfast in your own time. (The quid pro quo is that you don't have to mind when dinner is a bit late.)

In the bar is a Bakelite phone and a one-handed clock that declares "oneish, twoish, threeish...". Wry, real, and refreshing. Evelyn Waugh wrote in his diaries: 'Punctuality is the virtue of the bored.' Nobody should be bored here – so what does it matter?

Richard & Sheila Johnston

Fingals,
Combe, Dittisham, TQ6 0JA
- 11 rooms £80-£170.
- Barn for 4 £600-£900 p.w.
- Dinner £30.
- 01803 722398
- www.fingals.co.uk
- Train station: Totnes

Agaric Rooms at Tudor House

DEVON

People come to Agaric as much for what it lacks – a frenetic environment, foams and dribbles on dining plates, wi-fi, Sky, huge plasma screens – as for what it has: a sense of comfort, authenticity and well-being. "Most importantly, we provide an atmosphere in which people relax," explains Sophie. "When they arrive, we want them to feel that they're in safe hands."

Nick (the chef) and Sophie (everything else) have such passion that you could never doubt the experience will be good. But there's also a life-affirming whiff of rebellion and joie de vivre about them – they take off with their three children, in wetsuits, to cook mussels for breakfast on the beach – so you can almost guarantee it will be fun, too.

Nick earned his cheffing stripes at Dartmouth's celebrated The Carved Angel. Sophie (a designer and artist) was passing through on her way from Scotland to the Pyrenées, discovered Dartmoor, and then discovered Nick who happily shared her interests in food, foraging and the outdoor life. Combining their creative strengths, they opened Agaric in 2000, in a sturdy, granite, sixteenth-century cottage in the centre of Ashburton which Sophie says is "a proper farming town with real roots".

Four years later, they bought the run-down Georgian townhouse next-door-but-one and converted its dingy bed-sit layout into a bed

and breakfast with five dashing bedrooms. You might find a roll-top bath, deep purple walls, Oriental lacquered bed or an art deco fireplace; Sophie's unerring eye is evident everywhere, as is her flair for breathing new life into salvaged furniture from the local skip.

They refused to put televisions in the rooms but relented when it was pointed out that some guests might not have the same "anti-TV" mind-set as they do. Now some of the rooms have them – and Roberts radios and beautiful books – and youngest daughter Millie loves to find an empty room on Saturday mornings to watch television.

They are ridiculously spoilt for fresh local produce. "Most of our supplies come from within twenty miles. Fish comes off the day-boats sailing out of Brixham; deer and pigeon are shot on local land. "We're very lucky that we've still got a local abattoir," says Nick. "Our meat never travels more than ten miles." One of their cheese suppliers has his own 'cave', plus they grow salads and herbs in the cottagey garden behind the restaurant.

Their bolthole is an eight-acre field in a valley close by. "There we have a lovely old caravan where we retreat to sculpt, build and dig."

They've planted a traditional orchard and have trees heavy with quinces, medlars, mulberries, plums, pears, apples, cherries and elderberries and soft fruits such as loganberries and

blackcurrants. In a fit of energetic optimism they planted olive trees (hardy northern European varieties) that they have shielded by windbreaks and have plans for vines. "We get weather off the Atlantic and it can be windy but the trees have strong roots." Sophie grows sweet peas and dahlias for the restaurant and the bedrooms.

The fruits go into jams, preserves, sauces and puddings. Nothing is bought ready-made; everything from breads to ice-cream, pâtes to fudge, is made here. Nick has even built a wood-fired oven to smoke meats and fish and bake bread.

Menus are led by what's growing and are about flavour and reinvigoration of flavour through clever combinations. In summer there might be grilled turbot with sorrel hollandaise and grilled fennel while an autumn pudding could be a soufflé of locally grown Pixy apples with brandy ice cream. A favourite starter is warm pigeon breast with raspberry vinegar, smoked bacon and mustard leaves.

Rugs on polished floorboards, low ceilings, flickering candles, bare wooden tables, crisp napkins and a sumptuous velvet settee in the small bar area create an atmosphere that embraces diners. Across the courtyard is their newest venture: a demonstration kitchen which sits at the back of their new kitchen/deli shop. Here, Nick runs both hands-on workshops and demonstrations, or you can just breeze by on a Saturday and ask him for advice.

Ashburton is a place where people go shopping with a basket; in its high street every shop is independent. There are bakers, butchers, antique shops, a seed merchant, an ironmonger's.

Borrow one of Sophie's maps and explore Dartmoor. She will point you to Wistman's Wood, a magical ancient woodland of trees, moss-covered granite boulders with buzzards wheeling overhead. She will also reveal the whereabouts of their special beach with its miles of flat sand and shallow waters that teem with sea bass and skate.

They have no more spare time than the rest of us but Nick and Sophie take their pleasures simply. "We try to have as little impact as possible on the world around us," says Sophie. "We go down to our field, walk the dog, take on silly projects."

Sophie admits she is "slightly fanatical" about recycling. "Everything should have more than one function," she says. "It can't just be pretty, it should also be practical and preferably cheap. Nick has recently made me a potting shed out of sandbags!"

Keeping it all going, Sophie admits, is hard. Success and expansion also bring more problems. "We're a small Devon town so staffing is tricky. And people expect London standards." The increased bureaucracy – business rates, licence fees, endless regulations – can dent their natural passion and enthusiasm. After ten years, she says, they still have financial worries and work "unbelievably" long hours.

She is grateful they're not toiling after a dream. Their greatest joy – family and field apart – is "seeing people appreciate the thought that has gone into what we provide. I remember one Easter Sunday Nick had taken extra time to make the lady who was staying Hot Cross buns for breakfast. She had tears in her eyes. Little things can mean so much."

Sophie & Nick Coiley

Agaric Rooms at Tudor House,
36 North Street, Ashburton, TQ13 7QD
- 3 rooms.
- From £110. Singles £50
- 2-course lunch from £12.95. Dinner £32.
- 01364 654478
- www.agaricrestaurant.co.uk
- Train station: Newton Abbot

Beara Farmhouse

DEVON

In one of the sleepiest corners of Devon, Richard and Ann have turned a run-down farmhouse into the rambling and lovely home it now is. For eighteen long months they lived in boiler suits and boots, demolished walls, rescued cast-iron guttering from a hedge, turned the oak from a tumbledown cowshed into a quaintly charming porch and transferred the old stones from the cowshed to the terrace.

Their magical touch with old material reaches into every corner of the place. The farmhouse had three old 'shippons' – cowsheds. One is now Richard's second home and workshop; carpenter, joiner and restorer, he's in his element standing in a shallow pool of wood shavings giving new life to old things.

Have you ever met anyone who has bought an old forge? One day Richard spotted one for sale in the local paper and felt he had to buy it. A retired blacksmith now comes by once or twice a week, heating, banging and coaxing raw metal into twisted candlesticks and bold chandeliers.

Those whose imaginations are happiest in the simpler ways of previous centuries would be happy here. There is a sense of right, timeless values at every corner. Indeed, Richard – faced with the task of restoring these ancient cob buildings – went on

a course to learn how to do it authentically.

The money was spent before the restoration ended so they foraged for extra income – in a spirit of openness and fun rather than in worried desperation. They even took to 'beating' on the local shoot, and discovered a deep delight in the area around their house. It is full of hidden combes, thickets and hollows, and of strutting pheasants and partridge.

The closeness of the North Devon coastline adds a powerful voice to the place and for many guests is the gilding on the lily. You can brave the choppy boat trip to Lundy island – a stupendous granite outcrop off the Devon coast, just three and a half miles long, the best place in England to spot rare Manx shearwaters, kittiwakes and those clowns of the air – puffins.

There are two lovely bedrooms in the main house, and two more in the Old Shippon (plus kitchen). Up the oak stairs is a living area with a wood-burning stove and views over the pond and the unsullied landscape beyond; settle in and you'll not want to leave. A further shippon, 'Sparrows', (named after the chatterboxes that cluster in the jasmine round the door) has the same beautiful views.

As for 'Little Beara', this an engagingly eccentric stone playhouse for the grandchildren, where a tiny fire can toast both bread and feet. It was built by Ben, a young lad who came on work experience and who is now a fully-fledged stonemason. Other wry architectural gestures are the fully tiled pig shed and the half-timbered house 'for sale' by the fence, big enough to house half of one adult body or the free-ranging ducks and hens.

Part of the magic here is the clash of expectations. So deep is the rusticity of the life they lead that one expects a raw interior. But it is lovely, and in a sophisticated way. There is a subtle marriage of raw wood and old materials with modern ideas, all held together with a light ironic touch.

It is homely, too: Ann has delicately stencilled bedroom walls and scattered her own needlepoint cushions across pastel bedspreads. The tone is intimate and tender, affectionate towards anything that has value, shape and beauty. It is 'cottagey' rather than coy.

A slow rural life can only be slower and better with animals. There are enough of them here to make Richard look somewhat Noah-like at times, especially as they are so well housed. Reuben was the first Kune Kune pig, Reuben led to Ruby and then Parsley and Posy. Six Southdown sheep are growing fat in their easy role as lawnmowers along the farmhouse track.

It is easy to be here with Richard and Ann; they have not just accepted this life but are gaily immersed in it. There is no gulf between visitors and them, just a seamless and immediate connection; witness the humour with which they greeted immaculately dressed guests one day as they themselves were wrestling in the mud with errant pigs. And they have turned ordinary things, like a pile of flower pots, into 'objets d'amusement.'

Given such a generous welcome, guests often become good friends, returning year after year, appreciating their hosts' place in the community and the unusual home that they have created. "We've made more friends here in two years than in twenty-five in Essex, and with the B&B we are never lonely. We don't have to go anywhere to find

somewhere lovely to be; we just sit and look at the fields. Of course the pressures are still there – it's not some magic idyll where all your problems disappear. But we have chosen to be here and we don't have to work to the clock."

Compared to Essex, this corner of Devon is a hundred years in the past. "I went to hire some

"Part of the magic here is the clash of expectations"

machinery," explains Richard. "In Essex, they would have taken my picture and demanded a deposit. Here they said 'Deposit? What do you mean?' That's trusting, and hugely refreshing."

"We do know people that have moved here, then moved back as they can't stand the slowness," Ann says. "You do have to wait to get work done." Both of them seem wary of technology. "Richard doesn't know how anything works unless you can hit it with a hammer!" Ann adds affectionately. But this attitude comes with having a great many other things to do. "Our time is spent doing, not sitting in front of a screen." When they have a spare hour or two they'd rather read or paint, potter in the garden, or hunt down that elusive chunk of wood. Sophisticated living comes more easily, perhaps, without much technology.

Ann & Richard Dorsett

Beara Farmhouse,
Buckland Brewer, Bideford, EX39 5EH
- 2 B&B rooms, from £70. Singles by arrangement.
- 2 barns for 4, £300–£650 p.w.
- 01237 451666
- www.bearafarmhouse.co.uk
- Train station: Barnstaple

The Bull Hotel

DORSET

Bridport bustles, its little shops are busy and there's a real community spirit, especially on Wednesdays and Saturdays, market days, when the local farmers and producers set out their stalls – over a mile of them on Saturday – and charm townfolk and visitors into parting with their money in return for the best from Dorset's larder.

The Bull stands sentinel and has been revived from a tired old town hotel into a vibrant, friendly, hub of the community. You'll see local builders and fishermen drop in for a sandwich, families arriving with suitcases for the weekend and maybe the local forager arriving with a basket full of wild salad or mushrooms for the kitchen.

Richard and Nikki Cooper bought the hotel four years ago. They were music industry executives then, living some sort of high life but cherishing, more and more, their time between travelling. They were already living in Dorset and commuting to London when The Bull came onto the market and could sense an excitement building up around the town. Hugh Fearnley-Whittingstall played an enormous part in reviving Bridport's fortunes; River Cottage, ten miles away, draws thousands of visitors each year to its open days, courses and restaurant. The Coopers, entrepreneurs both, leapt in where many of us would have dithered and seized the opportunity to buy

the hotel and create a new career that would fit with family life.

"I was lucky enough to have eaten great food all over the world," says Richard, "and I harboured a passion for running a restaurant. I could see that having a hotel offered a way of achieving that: the revenue from the rooms is vital for running the kitchen in the way I want to."

The hotel that guests are so enjoying is full of stuff the Coopers have gathered, from auctions and markets, and their inspiration came from their holidays spent in privately-owned French châteaux. There are blousey floral wallpapers, delicate Japanese prints, carved armoires, four posters, gilded chairs and rolltop baths. The restaurant has a coastal feel and sofas, games and smiling staff encourage guests to unfurl. The dogs play their part too; borrow them for walks along the Jurassic coast or a wander around the harbour. If idle pursuits start to pall – as if – there are courses and masterclasses on basket weaving, drawing, fishing, woodworking. There's usually a member of staff willing to drop you at the start of your walk or scoop you up at the end. They'll arrange a picnic, too, and the overall impression is that you are in safe hands with your needs second-guessed. "It has taken us a long time to get The Bull just right. Now it's a reflection of who we are."

It wasn't always thus. The first version of their website did a good job of attracting lots of interested new customers but they weren't necessarily the people best suited. "We'd given the impression that we were slicker than we wanted to be, so we attracted a crowd that was expecting something like The Metropolitan in London. We adjusted things to emphasise that we're not perfect and slick but natural, rustic and quirky. You don't get five stars and frills but you do get an interesting experience."

The Coopers are undoubtedly Slow in their approach to food but this wasn't something they trumpeted at first. "I didn't see why we needed to tell people we sourced locally; it seemed patronising," says Richard. Marketing logic decreed he should, of course, and his website now sports a charming gallery of suppliers: the fisherman, the forager, the butcher, the sheep farmer.

There is a self-effacing charm about Richard. He knows his limits and accepts they don't always get it right. "We're in some very smart guides," he says, "and sometimes I reckon we're the least polished place in them."

The hotel is not a money-making machine. "Our margins are rubbish, but we're happy and our integrity is intact." Even so they have to be guided by market forces. For example, they buy imported mozzarella for their legendary stonebaked pizzas, otherwise they would cost around fifteen pounds.

The Stable off the courtyard serves local ales, over fifty ciders, pizzas, pies and salads and has been a phenomenal success. They created a special dough with live yeast but only managed to make it on the first day; demand was so overwhelming they had to sub-contract the job to Leakers bakers opposite.

Using seasonal produce is wearing at times. "In winter we start running out of options and there's a collective sigh of relief when something new comes in – maybe the first purple sprouting or asparagus."

The Head Chef, Marc Montgommery, came from Marco Pierre White's Talkhouse and creates food events. There are moules and frites on Wednesday, canapés on Friday, brunch on market days and, all week, home-baked bread, cakes and scones. The

courtyard, set about with bunting and flowers, bustles at teatime and on warm summer evenings.

"I miss aspects of my old life in the music industry," Richard says, "but I got to the point when I was sitting in meetings with a room full of people with very strange haircuts and realised I was past it.

"When people arrive we can see in their eyes they are desperate for a break and are finding things tough. The staff look after them and they relax. I worked in the music industry for twenty years but this job is better, even, than that."

Bridport residents are enjoying the revived Bull, too. Local artists display their work, the Literary Festival is sponsored by The Bull and builders, architects and furniture-makers have all played their part in the look. "I'm pleased that we can contribute to the local economy," says Richard. "We all work together and play cricket together. We're now part of the furniture and we're here for the long haul."

The Bull Hotel

Nikki & Richard Cooper,
34 East Street, Bridport, DT6 3LF
- 15 rooms.
- £80-£260.
- Lunch & dinner. £5.50-£38.
- 01308 422878
- www.thebullhotel.co.uk
- Train station: Dorchester

North Wheddon Farm

SOMERSET

There are times, such as when grappling with a runaway ram intent on having its lustful way with next-door's ewes, when Julian Abraham wonders why he gave up his modern home in Chippenham. "It's been tough, but just this morning we sat in the yard and watched the sun come up and reflected on how we have created a job that we're proud of. You can't put a value on being so close to nature."

The village of Wheddon Cross on Exmoor is exceptionally peaceful. Just a quarter of a mile down a bumpy lane you come to an Arcadian England of fields, hills and hedgerows and, tucked in the lee of a wooded hill, the handsome Georgian North Wheddon Farm. Other than glimpses of the neighbouring farm, nothing comes between you and Dunkery Beacon. Kenny the cockerel, Lily the goose and Roxy the pygmy goat; pigs, sheep, lambs, chickens and dogs roam patches of the farm's twenty acres.

Before they came here the Abrahams had no idea how to tackle a ram, move a two-hundred-kilogram pig or help a ewe give birth. "We were too busy to think of much outside of our everyday life," says Julian, who was then running a restaurant, while Rachael, a home economist, worked in product development for a pasta company. "We had three children, but little opportunity for time together as a family. We decided that we wanted to work from home and wanted to grow our own good quality food. To set up something like this felt like an impossible dream and everyone thought we were unhinged: three kids under five, no experience of farming..."

They began searching in Exmoor because Julian had happy memories of family holidays there and after two years of looking and another two years of renovations they opened North Wheddon to guests. While Rachael tussled with her new role of looking after B&B guests and self-caterers in the cottages, Julian began his "real journey" of learning to farm.

"It began with two Saddleback pigs: I brought them home in my car. I quickly learned that working with animals, you have to go at their pace and work with them. I did a lot of my learning from books – not something I would recommend – and drew on the tremendous support of our neighbours."

Their collection of animals now includes Exmoor Horn Sheep, Gloucester Old Spots, Oxford Sandy Blacks, Muscovy ducks, ex-battery chickens, geese and, at Easter and Christmas, turkeys. Cattle is their next challenge – if they can buy a few more acres.

What they offer is the sort of place they would like to go to: somewhere to relax with comfy sofas, log fires, decent wines and good food. You will want to join in, to collect eggs for breakfast, smoke salmon in a marvellous dustbin and coathanger contraption, bottle-feed the lambs, even help with lambing (some guests time their holidays especially).

They are committed to boosting their local economy. "If we can't produce it ourselves, we buy local," says Julian. "If we can't buy locally, we have to decide whether to compromise. Bananas and lemons we find hard to resist but most of our cooking is a home game." They serve their own mutton, lamb and poultry, their own sausages, bacon, air-dried hams and salamis (hung for two years in an open-sided barn), preserves, ice creams and breads. They grow salads and vegetables and gather mushrooms from the fields.

Food is honest and tasty, perhaps smoked salmon and lemon mayonnaise followed by local venison or mutton and minted dumplings and rounded off with crispy pancakes and caramelised apples. If they're busy, the two older children, Holly and Ellie, help, too.

Rooms are homely: rugs on carpets, thick curtains, deep sofas and colourful bedspreads. Farthingwood Barn, the larger of the two self-catering places, has a vast kitchen table perfect for big gatherings; Eden Lodge, tucked in the eaves of the farmhouse, has beams and snug hideaways.

Living in a listed building in a National Park, the Abrahams cannot install double glazing and solar panels could be an issue. "We don't mind the restrictions as they are there to protect the

environment we live in," says Julian. "We're looking at a bio-mass boiler and a dowser has been to help us in our ambition to have our own borehole." It's an elemental place – the garden is criss-crossed with springs – and the atmosphere works its magic on tightly-wound guests. "It takes twenty-four hours for them to chill out," says Julian. "They fret at first about mobile reception being slack and in no time at all they are delighted."

You can take one of Rachael's picnics and a thermos and set off from the farmyard to lose yourself in Snowdrop Valley or Bossington Beach near Porlock. The fishing harbour in Porlock is the place for a stroll, Dunkery Beacon, with its views to Wales, perfect for a leg-stretching hike. Maps, wellies, extra children's jackets can all be borrowed.

Julian says they want to give people space to be still and breathe. "We say don't plan; just let it happen. Even if all they have done is help with a stuck sheep or fed the pigs, people value the experience and can take away a sense of another type of life."

Rachael & Julian Abraham

North Wheddon Farm,
Wheddon Cross, TA24 7EX
- 3 rooms. Doubles £77.
- Self catering available.
- Dinner £24.
- 01643 841791
- www.northwheddonfarm.co.uk
- Train station: Taunton

Royal Oak Inn

SOMERSET

Luxborough is in the Exmoor National Park, in a green sheltered valley between the Brendon and Croydon Hills, close to rugged moorland and woodland. Pub and village are right on the Coleridge Way that runs from Nether Stowey to Porlock on the coast – twenty-two miles from the start and a perfect overnight stopping point.

James Waller knew nothing about pubs but was desperate to get out of London, where he worked in the frenzied money markets. Why a pub, when the work is even harder? Ah, but the work is rewarding and this pub is special. Pubs can play a major role in the life of a village, especially now that so many other aspects of village life have been taken from us. Their landlords are key figures.

"I was working in the City. Running a pub was the last thing on my mind. But my son Eddie was three and I was leaving home at 5.30am and getting back at eight. I entertained clients on Saturdays and spent Sundays exhausted.

"We wanted to change direction and to be closer to our parents. I wanted to buy the type of place we like to go to: olde worlde, quiet, atmospheric – this!" There are no fruit machines, no background music, no pool table, no mobile reception – just a dartboard and a quiz league and,

occasionally, a cow or tractor trundling past.

The Royal Oak, a cider and perry pub, goes back five hundred years. The Back Bar was once the local abattoir; meat hooks are still visible in the beams. The butcher also plied his trade here, with a small shop near the well (they still get water from their spring in the cellar) and, until the sixties, there was a bar for women only.

Even the local tailor, a Mr Spiller, had workrooms in what are now bedrooms, and the village shop and post office were here until twelve years ago. 'Progress' has removed them, though a new village hall has been built.

Two intimate low-beamed bars lead to a warren of dining rooms decked with polished tables and hunting prints on dark walls. A shelf heaves with walking books and maps, lent freely. "People come to walk, to sit by the fire, to do nothing. They go to bed early – the fresh air gets to them." (Bedrooms ramble around the first floor: individual, peaceful and homely.)

During the shooting season the bar hums with the sound of gamekeepers, beaters, drivers and picker-uppers from the nearby Chargot shoot. Shooting is a deep-rooted part of the local scene, and very convivial. "The shoot (pheasants and partridges) has been coming down for at least ten years. At lunchtime it's the beaters,

picker-uppers and loaders. They all have their set tables. It's a great atmosphere. They come in from the beginning of September until the end of January, and have their own back room to dine in.

"I'd never pulled a pint before we arrived. When we took over on the first day of January 2002, it was the last day of the shooting season and I had ninety in for lunch. In the first three months of being here my feet hardly touched the ground I lost two stone!"

The spirit of the place has worked its magic on the once-overwrought James.

"My wife Sîan goes up to London to work, but spends as much time here as she can. She does the

> "People play cribbage,
> backgammon, scrabble.
> The locals talk and drink.
> The dogs doze by the fire"

breakfasts, and the flowers. It is the most wonderful place to bring up children. Ed is twelve now and goes off on his bike with his friends. Everyone in the village knows him. The school bus picks him up from the door.

"We have kept the basic format. The village is small but people have been coming here all their lives. People play cribbage, backgammon, scrabble. The locals talk and drink. The dogs doze by the fire."

James's commitment to local life is shown by his attitude to the regulars: there's one big table right by the fire, reserved every evening of the year just for them. One seat in particular is reserved for Dennis, who has been drinking amiably here for eighteen years and has his portrait on the wall.

James inherited Tim Sandy as head chef. He was trained in London and later worked at Bentley's the seafood restaurant, hence the Royal Oak's emphasis on fish, alongside game. The menu changes seasonally, with daily specials too. The beef, lamb and venison almost walk off the hills

into the kitchen. "When I have the roast lamb on a Sunday I can point out to our diners the chap who grew their lamb."

The fish comes from St Mawes in Cornwall. Soups and puddings are homemade. In the inter-connecting Green and Red Rooms diners are encouraged to take their time, and have the table for the whole evening, an unusual touch.

The beer is as local as possible and so are the two scrumpy ciders: Thatcher's Cheddar Valley and Rich's. "If I change the beer there is widespread outcry! And you have to have cider in a Somerset pub."

It is marvellous to stay and eat at an inn whose landlord is so contented with his lot. "I'm hands on, and have Anita, who is a godsend. I'm my own man here, setting my own agenda. I enjoy meeting people and everyone has time to talk. We've made more friends in eight years here than we did in twenty in London. Within two days of arriving we knew the postman's name. The hours are long, but I'm not answerable to anyone. And the staff are so friendly; everyone helps each other."

In the next year or so the Coleridge bridleway will be complete. There are stables near the Royal Oak and James is putting up tethering posts to the side so that thirsty riders can pop in for a drink.

Exmoor is stunning at all times of the year. It is almost as wild and beautiful as England can get. The Royal Oak gilds the lily – magnificently.

James & Siân Waller

Royal Oak Inn,
Luxborough, Watchet, TA23 0SH
- 11 rooms. £75–£100.
- Main courses £11.95–£16.95. Bar meals from £4.95.
- 01984 640319
- www.theroyaloakinnluxborough.co.uk
- Train station: Taunton

Binham Grange

SOMERSET

The M5 that spirits crowds of us to Devon and Cornwall gently releases others to slip away quietly and head for the little-sung hills of Somerset. Here, between the Quantocks and the Brendon Hills, you can settle into the slow delights of Binham Grange.

Comfortable beds, log fires, clear night skies, seeing what's new in the garden, honest food and simple, unaffected hospitality – they are simple pleasures and, for Marie, the quintessence of going slow. She and her husband Stewart are a dynamic, hard-working couple; they ran a dairy farm in Carmarthenshire for over thirty years, raised three children, ran a restaurant, were garden designers and involved in restoration at Aberglasney gardens, known as the 'Heligan of Wales'.

In 2002, the National Trust of Wales wanted to buy the family farm in Carmarthenshire and so began a search for an equally special spot elsewhere. Binham Grange, a Grade II*-listed Jacobean mansion, came into view. It was empty and dilapidated with concrete in the fields, blocked-up fireplaces, gardens of leylandii. The leylandii would have been enough to deter the bravest souls, but the whole place was a challenge. Somehow it seemed to deserve support.

They couldn't resist. Once they moved in, Tudor alabaster friezes were uncovered, cornices repaired, lime plaster mixed, oak floors and doors reinstated, and their pedigree herd of Holstein Friesians installed in the three hundred acres of farmland. Gardens and terraces were magicked out of the unpromising grass bordered with the leylandii: a formal parterre, a rose pergola leading to an Italian-style garden, kitchen garden and orchard. They opened for business at Christmas 2006 with just two bedrooms for visitors, and a restaurant. Daughter Victoria, gifted with her mother's love of cooking, helps run the show. "Our aim was simply to do what we enjoy: cooking, gardening and looking after people - with the bonus of helping to sustain our countryside."

It's this simplicity of approach, albeit on a grand scale, that makes Binham Grange work. The restaurant prepares 'simple food simply' because, as Marie points out, "the ingredients are excellent". The two bedrooms are an invitation to rest with soft colours, antique furniture, Hungarian goose-down quilts, books, magazines, a roll-top bath in one, a magnolia creeping up to the window of the other.

The murmuring restlessness of the sea, even though it's two fields away, can be heard as you wake. "It's so quiet here," says Marie, "you can hear the tide turning." After a gentle awakening, you breakfast on home-baked bread, milk from their dairy – a very rare treat these days – homemade jams and marmalades, locally churned butter, free-range eggs from 'Jill-on-the-Hill' and bacon, sausages and pork from the next-door farm. It is all quite delicious.

Hikes on Exmoor are a delight for walkers, or take the gentle Church Walk, created by the monks of nearby Cleeve Abbey, down to Blue Anchor Bay. Stroll along the coast and catch one of the steam trains on the West Somerset Railway for the return journey. Marie does an excellent picnic and can send you off with maps.

If you've chosen not to move for the day, afternoon teas on the terrace or by the fire fill that languorous gap between lunch and dinner. On some days, Marie organises a 'vintage afternoon tea', with antique bone china and cakes and drop scones baked on the Aga. "I like the history of cookery. We've over three-hundred cookery books in the kitchen which we dip in to, from Marguerite Patten to Jamie Oliver."

Cakes and puddings are Victoria's speciality, whether it's traditional Welsh Bara Brith, an Eton Mess in June or blackberry crumble in October. A favourite with guests is lemon posset which they serve with a shot of limoncello and lemon shortbread and decorate with a tiny flower from the garden.

Ingredients – if you'll excuse the lemons – are sourced from within twenty miles. Organic fruits, herbs and seasonal vegetables are from their own patch or from neighbouring farms, cheese and clotted cream made from their own milk at the local dairy, meat and game from Exmoor farms and

estates. A smokery on the Somerset Levels supplies cured fish and meat, there are soft drinks from Luscombe at nearby Buckfastleigh and Somerset apple brandy too. Jackie, the fish merchant who lives on Exmoor, travels to Brixham after a 4am start and is handing Marie the overnight catch by 11am.

Nothing ready-prepared is allowed to enter the kitchen, and there is no outside help so holidays are a rarity for Marie and Victoria. They really do prefer to be here, though, making guests drinks to have on the terrace and enjoying their appreciation of dinners around the oak tables. There are quiet moments, even for them, around the fire or taking in the sunset over North Hill.

Apart from running the farm, the rooms, the restaurant and the garden (where Marie concedes they have a little help), they have garden open days and tea-tasting specials, hold exhibitions of local art, put on theatrical performances in the garden and find time to pop to the station to pick up guests.

"Some days are hard," concedes Marie. "I enjoy the restaurant and people, but in dairy farming you work so hard for so little."

Marie and Stewart have an infectious way of appreciating the natural world. Getting up early, day after day, to tend to the animals and guests is a hard discipline, Marie agrees, "but I love to get out of bed to see what's growing in the garden and watch the sunset from the kitchen window. At times it just stops us. It's a joy and is different every day." If only most of us could capture the same magic in our daily lives. Perhaps we could.

Marie Thomas

Binham Grange,
Old Cleeve, Minehead, TA24 6HX
* 2 rooms. £100-£140.
* Dinner, £30.
* 01984 640056
* www.binhamgrange.com
* Train station: Blue Anchor

Huntstile Organic Farm

SOMERSET

"This is a happy, loving house," is Lizzie's opening remark, "we are so very lucky." The tone is set.

On a sloping site in the rolling green foothills of the Quantocks, among stands of oak, beech, hazelnut and lime trees that prosper in the rich red loam, she and John are doing what they want to do, with energy and pleasure. "There are so many magical moments, such as the two weeks in May when the limes make a new green canopy over the carpet of bluebells, the delicate scent of the pea flowers and fresh 'green-ness' of summer, and this contrasts with the wonderful russet tones of autumn and big fat round bales of hay, that cast their long shadows across the stubble field".

It is an ancient land. The beautiful hills rise from the low-lying Somerset Levels, the footprint of a prehistoric inland sea, and Somerset swarms with history and legend. Glastonbury Abbey was said to have been founded by Joseph of Arimathea when he brought the Holy Grail to England; legend also has it that King Arthur and Queen Guinevere are buried here. We 'know' that Alfred the Great, preoccupied with kingly worries, let a batch of cakes burn in a peasant's hovel on the Somerset Levels.

From pagan times, hand-fastings must have been held in these deeply rural reaches. Leaping over the centuries, this rustic

celebration of coupledom can now be performed at Huntstile, in the hilltop stone circle that Lizzie and John have built with old staddle stones, that gazes across the land to Bridgwater Bay.

"John is a brilliant farmer," says his wife. "He was born into generations of inherited skills and instinctively knows about the soil, the seasons, when to sow and when to reap. "He's a natural biodynamic practitioner. Working a total of 650 acres, mostly arable and virtually on his own these days, John started as a conventional farmer. He was converted by Lizzie, whose small-holding experience had convinced her that the land needed to be clean, and his brother-in-law, whose organic box scheme was a huge success. The lesson began to make economic as well as environmental sense. He and Lizzie realised that to save Huntstile they needed to make both his beloved family house and the land pay their way. Organic crops would sell for a better price and they would devote the conversion years to renovating the house. "Its wonderful atmosphere is now shared with the people who come and stay, come for a party or a course – this is what we wanted."

They began by removing the 1950s modernisations: plaster everywhere, asbestos ceilings, Crittall windows, 'period' tiles, woodchip wallpaper in a house that was built in 1430, during the reign of Henry VI – and revealed such treasures that they knew it was worth it. There were huge beams and fireplaces, superb fourteen-inch-wide elm floorboards, Jacobean oak panelling with a frieze of Tudor roses and fern leaves in the sitting room – marvels of all sorts. John found a quill pen from the 1800s belonging to an A. Danger' (whom they later discovered was using a similar crop rotation to their own); a pair of seventeenth-century shoes had been hidden under one floorboard and lots of coins; a traveller's diary from 1688, discovered in a crack. "These links to the past nourish us all," says Lizzie, "and when you add fresh, uncontaminated food, long lovely views, glorious walks and a wildlife lake, the whole person jubilates." People can wander over the whole farm, there are no restrictions.

The renovation work was done by John, Lizzie, some of the five sons they have between them, and the unstinting help of a couple of Polish men who turned up one day on their bicycles, looking for weekend work. "Radek & Kamil were reliable, hard-working and could turn their hand to any job – welding, plumbing, masonry; we couldn't have done it without the help of our East European friends." It's a bit like the United Nations on the farm these days, with Swedish, South African, Latvian, Thai and Polish helpers turning their hands to working in the kitchen, driving the tractor or loading corn in the grain barn. The house now has seven cosily rustic bedrooms for guests and two beautiful reception rooms.

Food is all locally produced and organic wherever possible, either home grown in the wonderful kitchen garden, or from Lizzie's favourite local suppliers – there being four other organic growers within five miles of Huntstile. "Vegetable growing is time- and labour-intensive but well worth the effort for the wonderful flavours produced," she says. "The varieties we grow in our kitchen garden are chosen purely for their delicious flavours, I dream of one day producing whole farm-grown meals with Huntstile lamb, pork, beef, chicken, vegetables, salads, herbs, eggs and fruit – maybe soon Huntstile will see the return of a Jersey house cow, like the one

that John's father used to keep ('Miranda') in the orchard, providing milk and cream for breakfast."

Having sold his cattle, John is planning to have a flock of sheep as they are more suited to the whole farm organic rotation. Lizzie's dream is coming closer. Once the conversion to organic systems was achieved, John found that his arable skills were, if possible, enhanced. He grows organic spelt for a local company in Shepton Mallet, organic wheat, oats, beans, rye grass and clover for hay and silage to feed organic beef and dairy herds. "It's good for the soil structure and we collect our own organic seeds." And he's finding, after five years, that the market is coming to him with requests for new crops.

After a visit to the Paris Agricultural Show, he is considering producing his own bio-diesel for the tractors and a bio-mass wood-fired boiler is on the programme for 2010. "We have a small piece of woodland on our farm, and the hedges are now being allowed to mature for several years producing a good crop of sustainable firewood".

Meanwhile, Lizzie does all she can to spread the word about buying from local producers. "We host the Slow Food Market every Wednesday which is a marvellous showcase for local produce, freshly baked bread, organic cream teas, barbecue local meats and takeaway salads and we also do local food events to introduce people to the local growers. The food is usually donated free, contributions go to a local charity and connections are made." Lizzie and John shine with their delight in life, Huntstile and the rewards of living in this beautiful place.

Lizzie Myers

Huntstile Organic Farm,
Goathurst, Bridgwater, TA5 2DQ
- 5 rooms.
- From £79. Singles from £49
- Dinner 2 courses £15-£20, 3 courses £20-£25.
- 01278 662358
- www.huntstileorganicfarm.co.uk
- Train station: Bridgwater

Church Cottage

SOMERSET

Caroline discovered the little cottage eight years ago, then decided to start B&B. It's a brilliant spot, a great stopping off point for the South West, lying in the Somerset Levels where the unforgettable Glastonbury Tor rises out of the morning mist. It's also right on the cycle route from John O' Groats to Land's End – though it would be a shame not to linger here, walking the lanes and wetlands, spotting the wildlife and the birds.

At the bottom of Caroline Hanbury Bateman's garden is the Potting Shed, a bolthole for two, from whose warmly dressed bedroom window a fourteenth-century church tower is framed. It is surely the best turned-out potting shed in England. Have your Aga-cooked breakfast brought to you here – there's a little round table for two – or wander over to the cottage and pull up a chair by the big pine table, bought years ago in Dublin and full of memories of life with four young sons. Caroline is a fantastic cook and is happy to rustle up anything for you from kedgeree and Welsh rarebit to Spanish omelette, however the mood takes you. What is not to be missed is her earthy, moist soda bread with its bubbly crust. The dough is deliciously elastic, "a doddle to make".

Caroline's is a serene and happy cottage, with a bright,

uncluttered interior and an immaculately tended cottage-style garden that wraps itself around the house at the back and to one side. About 15 roses grow along a wall abutting the churchyard, in a bed sprinkled with tulips and bulbs in spring, and foxgloves, dahlias and variegated euphorbia in summer; on the south-facing wall of the house are tender plants such as lemon verbena and a red abutillon. Climbing French beans stand to attention among the flowerbeds – they work harder than runner beans, as they crop time and again and can withstand a drought – and the first freesias she's ever grown outdoors suggest warmer summers to come. Elsewhere, sweet peas flourish.

"Once you've got wild rocket in the ground you never need another packet," says Caroline. And here it's left to spread its bounty among the other plants, creating easy ground cover and a brilliant green manure – as well as being exceptionally tasty. The generously proportioned lawn is undulated: Caroline prefers it that way.

A lifetime of adventures began when Caroline and her mother headed for Africa on a troop ship just after the war. Spending her childhood on an isolated farm in Kenya, electricity-free, life was simple. "My Mother was rather ahead of her time and believed in the power of fresh food. She said

the only household items she bought were loo paper and sugar. As we lived forty miles from the nearest township, and the roads to that were impassable in the rains, it was just as well she was practical." In Somerset, Caroline nurtures that ethos. "Our food is local wherever possible, and organic. I make my own bread, grow a lot of vegetables in the garden among the flowers, and always have fresh flowers in the house."

Caroline's past life has turned her into her own 'mother of invention'. Returning to England her life took yet more turns. She trained as a cook, learnt the wine trade, went gardening, raised four boys. "Skills start at home and they're instinctively in you," and the family always sat down together to eat. "Breakfast was a bit rushed, packed lunch was at school, but supper was sharing and chatting time. I feel sorry for families that, for whatever reason, don't – it only takes one hour of the day and possibly less if everyone joins in the preparation."

No processed food was bought, no microwaves used, everything was fresh and cooked daily. "We grew our own vegetables, had hens for eggs, and made bread. Because I'm a hopeless and

disinterested pudding maker, puddings rarely appeared. I did feel slightly chastened when some of the boys' friends came home for supper, and to show willing I'd made a milk jelly. This was the height of excitement for them, but sniffed at by their friends!"

All the boys are good, imaginative cooks now, great believers in the power of fresh and 'real' food. One has his own pie business, The Square Pie Company, in London, selling at Spitalfields and Selfridges; all are self-employed.

A stint in West Cork heightened Caroline's foodie passion, where the Slow Food movement is in full force. But her version is slightly more "hands on and everyday" – a more English approach. She prides herself on being quite possibly the only woman in England to have never been to a takeaway.

"It doesn't appeal to me. You miss out on the conviviality and the atmosphere. Added to that I do like to know what is going into my food and wonder if you can trust a restaurant that is trying to serve those inside and those wanting to take food away."

Caroline's Slow style spills over into that lovely walled garden, peaceful and secluded in spite of

being in the middle of a popular village. Shapwick is a 'blue lias' Polden Hill village, surrounded by farmland and overlooking the Somerset Levels. For those who prefer higher altitudes, the Quantocks and the Mendips are not far; so are Glastonbury and Wells. Wells is the smallest cathedral city in England, home to the Bishop's Palace (gardens, moat and swans) and to markets galore: open-air markets twice a week, and a wonderful farmers' market every Wednesday.

The cottage, with its polished old flagstones and chunky beams, has a history. Not so very long ago, ten children would have been raised in one part and the rest given over to peat. Later it became a doctor's surgery. Now the house is warm, countrified and cosy – a whiff of woodsmoke in autumn, floppy roses in June. Very English – but with an 'out of Africa' touch: note the carvings, paintings and the bronze sculpture of a cheetah peering out over his savannah. The bedroom is small and simple – pine furniture, cool colours – while the Potting Shed is a wonderfully private nest for two.

The new oak staircase was constructed by a village builder; the odd sloping floor and wonky wall add to the charm; the vintage 'Vacant' sign on the loo door gives a quirky touch, and the bathrooms are simple and restful.

Caroline has many traditional skills to pass on. Her youngest son tells her she should write it all down – day to day, what she does and how. For now... relish her house and garden, accept her lightly chilled rosé as the sun goes down, wander off to the lichen-dusted bench at the end of the garden, and raise a glass to a simple life in the slow lane.

Caroline Hanbury Bateman

Church Cottage,
Station Road,
Shapwick, Bridgwater, TA7 9NH
- 2 rooms. £70-£85. Singles £60-£75.
- Packed lunch on request.
- 01458 210904
- www.churchcottageshapwick.co.uk
- Train station: Bridgwater

Barwick Farm House

SOMERSET

Ask Angela "Why Barwick?" and she will reply: "Because it was really old and brilliantly derelict! I grew up in a smart country house which had everything it could need for perfection. Those days a lot of the gardening was done with chemicals which killed all the wild things: it broke my heart." That was where Angela grew her desire to protect the earth and her undying love of horses and riding. "My dream was to do up an old house in the old way with natural materials and buckets of limewash. I had lived in Greece in winter and knew that earth floors covered with slabs of stone not only work, they are beautiful, too. The ground floor, in our part of the house, has huge old flags. I love the way they tell the years." One is quickly caught up in her passion for the buildings and the land, their history and heart is infectious.

The house had been lived in by tenant farmers since it was built. Angela and Robin brought it into the third millenium while saving its genuine farm atmosphere – and its soul. Their light-handed restoration returned it to a simpler structure with just enough modernisation to make it warm and properly plumbed, the rooms being done with modern breathable sealers and paints. There is no formal garden, just rough land with the ewes coming up to the front door with their lambs.

The land they put back to work as an old-fashioned smallholding. They raise rare Dorset sheep, hens, horses and all the attendant wildlife: heron and ducks are often seen on the two streams that run through the land, the foxes carried off several flocks of hens before they put in electric fencing. "I observe what grows, how and where, and I don't mind scruffy. We're not planning anything smart, no posh trees, but we're tweaking things to make it prettier, such as the view through the alders by the stream, over the top of the eighteenth-century pigsties. I simply love unregenerate old farm buildings: we'll re-roof the fallen bays and leave it at that."

They sowed a £91 bag of seeds in some of the fields to create a wildflower conservation project. It is already beautiful, full of wild things, and in a few years will cover the whole area. They are living through the pleasures and pains of kitchen gardening, too. The first year, they turned over a huge nettle bed, planted and sowed and, to their astonishment, reaped prizes for their organic produce. The second year, the slugs arrived and there were no prizes. "But we wouldn't dream of using non-organic antidotes."

Angela says of her husband: "Robin has been abroad most of his adult life, working with aid agencies and public bodies; he's civilised and lovely and likes reading. He knew he wanted to end up in the country, though, and has converted to life at Barwick with a vengeance and enjoys playing with new toys like the chainsaw."

The local community has been part of the project from the outset. Having brought up three stepchildren and three of her own, Angela cares about the young. While she toiled away at making the place habitable she invited a village teenage band to practise in the magnificently raftered barn (now the splendid holiday flat). "The boys helped lots,

> "We have under-repaired these fabulous original boards, exposing their age and we used the elm planks that were the old feed bins to make a dining table for the main house"

and one youngster helps muck out our horses. He is rebuilding an ancient Fergie tractor – I can't wait to use it." Robin and Angela have a great party with these allies every August.

They both sing in the local choir, bass and soprano respectively. "I was pushed to join by my lovely daughter, then found I could do it myself. I took her place when she went up to Oxford on a choral scholarship." Angela finds little time to paint now. "The house is hung with works by our two fathers, our grandmothers, my children – all my good stuff is in other people's houses... I would love to fit painting back into my life some time."

For "the nearest good pub meal," the Nicoll's send their guests to East Coker, the village that seventy years ago inspired the second of T. S. Eliot's still evocative Four Quartets (he's buried there too):

> In my beginning is my end. In succession
> Houses rise and fall, crumble, are extended,
> Are removed, destroyed, restored, or in their place
> Is an open field, or a factory, or a by-pass.

This is rural Somerset, where riding and hunting are part of life. Angela trained show ponies, starting raw beginners quietly and slowly by example: she mounts her own horse and leads the newcomer round companionably until rider and tack have become normal. "Only ten years ago," she says, "I reschooled a big chestnut thoroughbred and competed with him – as a senior, you understand – and hunted him sidesaddle. We can't afford to hunt here for the moment..."

The idiosyncratic elms that once stood tall along the lanes of Somerset are no more, felled by a pernicious twentieth-century strain of Dutch elm disease, but Barwick Farm House keeps quantities of big elm floorboards safe and sound; they were cut from trees that were mature four hundred years ago. "We have under-repaired these fabulous original boards, exposing their age: they had been misused and it shows. And we used the elm planks that were the old feed bins to make a dining table for the main house." Breakfast is in the library, however, which catches the morning sun leaning in over the farmyard. One trusted Yeovil butcher provides the sizzling bacon and sausages, Angela picks tasty mushrooms from the surrounding fields, jams are home-grown.

After this feast, sit in the sheltered farmyard, warm and peaceful among the hens. Or take off, maybe with a couple of the dogs, to explore the woods and valleys that surround Barwick.

Angela Nicoll

Barwick Farm House
Barwick, Yeovil, BA22 9TD
- 5 rooms: 3 in house, 2 in barn.
- £60-£90.
- Singles £40-£60.
- 01935 410779
- www.barwickfarmhouse.co.uk
- Train station: Yeovil Junction

Harptree Court

SOMERSET

Harptree Court, in the family for three generations, is at the centre of numerous village events. The Women's Institute is a grateful recipient of the Court's homemade cake, the Chew Valley Monday Club puts on its teas, the Church, its monthly suppers, the playgroup comes for a weekly ramble, and the East Harptree Orchestra plays on the lawns. Anyone who can play one bar of music is taken on, there are nineteen flutes, twenty-six clarinets, one French horn, three trombones, thirty violins, four cellos, fifteen recorders, fourteen saxophones, and any profits go to buy instruments for loan to young musicians.

Linda and Charles feel that ownership of such a huge house carries serious responsibilities, but they enjoy these events as much as anybody. One unusual project is the sharing of the big walled kitchen garden with a group of villagers who are allowed to use half of the garden for free, thus increasing the amount of organic fruit, flowers and vegetables available. The

walled garden is also the source of most of the fresh food served to B&B visitors. Jo and Annabel set up a table and sell bunches of sweet williams, sweet peas, red potatoes, asparagus, courgettes, beans and onions. It's a new project, and is growing apace in this walled space that keeps out rabbits and raises the temperature a couple of degrees. The concept of Slow is entirely familiar to those at Harptree, though perhaps here it is simply known as 'country life.'

Charles's grandfather bought the house in 1920, with money made from shipbuilding in Bristol. All Bristolians knew of the Charles Hill shipyard, just next to the 'ss Great Britain' and very much part of the Bristol tradition. Its slow demise was a cause of much sadness – the slow end of Bristol's long and proud history as a working harbour. But shipping did well after the First War and the Hill family lived in style. There were two grass tennis courts where the lily pond now is and grandfather would invite the Australian

tennis team to stay in the house and play with him when they were in Britain.

The house was also once a sort of local Hellfire Club, with gambling parties and frighteningly high stakes. It was not unknown for people to lose their houses but after one or two were seen searching the house for guns with which to shoot themselves after such losses, the gambling stopped. The twenties and thirties brought hard times; Charles's father and the family lived in one room, the Hall, with an open fire and no other heating.

Perhaps the experience reinforced a broader sense of community too. As well as providing green space for most of East Harptree's institutions, the Hills are active in the village – Charles has been a church warden and Linda was a Chairman of the school's PTA. The three children have grown and flown; Katie, a marine biologist, lives a few miles away.

The house itself is a classic of its kind, a big old Georgian manor house filled with fine furniture. From 1802 to 1875 the Waldegrave family owned it. It remains unchanged: un-grand, full of bonhomie and generosity, without a trace of pretension.

Much of this atmosphere must come from the fact that those three generations live here; Charles's mother is still a determined gardener and planter. She came from another Bristol trading family so she brought her own furniture with her, gilding an already handsome lily. You will find old rugs, candles, dark wooden floors made of purple heart wood from Trinidad, bells at the bottom of the stairs to ring when you are in need, flowers from the garden everywhere and a blazing open fire in winter.

As the Hills were shipbuilders they were able to bring those skills to the house; witness the brass screws in the floorboards. Upstairs there is a cosy sitting room for visitors, overlooking the croquet lawn. There are four splendid bedrooms for guests – Rust, Lavender, Pink and Yellow – all with fine, quiet views, heavy old family furniture and paintings. (The brolly and torch in each wardrobe are there to encourage you to walk to the village for a drink or dinner in the excellent pub.) The bathrooms are conventionally modern, and larger than they need be. Those belonging to the Rust and

Yellow rooms have the views, so you may be forgiven for lingering in the bath.

The garden is seventeen-acres huge – big enough for a 'Georgian' treehouse to hide in, and a luxurious yurt, projects due for completion in 2010. Look further and you find more: a folly, underground passage, ice house, waterfall, ha-ha, lake, clapper bridge, an old swimming pool that is now a lily pond filled with

> "A place for dreaming,
> for taking cream teas under
> a giant tree on the lawn"

goldfish... and a quarter mile of daffodils. Harptree is a place for dreaming, for playing croquet and tennis, for taking cream teas under a great tree on the lawn. The garden and woodland teem with wildlife; deer and woodpeckers are frequent visitors, a fox might trot past the window.

This is how a slice of English society lived right up to the First World War and beyond, a gentle life in a not-so-gentle age. For most people there was no choice between fast and slow, though 'fast' for the privileged few would have meant hectic partying, gambling, travelling up and down to London.

What you find here now are conviviality and community, local food generously served (their breakfast sausages are made for them, five miles away), the encouragement to 'be' rather than to rush, and a nourishing sense of connection with the past. In the words of one Irish visitor: "This is the best place we have ever stayed."

Linda Hill

Harptree Court,
East Harptree, Bristol, BS40 6AA
• 4 rooms. £110-£120.
• Singles £75-£80.
• Dinner £20-£25.
• 01761 221729
• www.harptreecourt.co.uk
• Train station: Castle Cary

The Griffin Inn

SUSSEX

"We do wine tastings on Tuesday evenings in winter, and gourmet dinners. There's live piano on Friday and some Saturday nights, and Sunday lunchtimes. There's cricket in summer and lots of different groups of locals meet together here in the evenings, too. We could turn it into a 'restaurant in the country', but that would distract from the fact that we are the oldest licensed premises in the south of England. We've had a continuous licence for five hundred years!"

The Griffin is a sixteenth-century inn overlooking the Ouse Valley in Fletching, a village with a lovely Norman church and old beamed buildings. Simon de Montfort prayed for victory in the church before the Battle of Lewes in 1264. In fact, that is how the village got its name: the soldiers "fletched" their arrows here on the eve of the battle. King Henry III lost, de Montfort won.

The countryside is gently undulating, the South Downs lie just to the south and Pooh Bear's favourite place is right here in Ashdown Forest. In fact, you can play Pooh Sticks from the bridge where Christopher Robin played the game. Traditions are faithfully adhered to in Sussex – as they are at The Griffin.

Cricket, for example, has its roots deep in Sussex soil. From the 1860s-1950s, the Australian

cricket team would stay with the Earl of Sheffield nearby. (Today you can visit Sheffield Park Gardens, famous for azaleas and rhododendrons.)

The Griffin has long views across to Sheffield Park and the Pullan family are cricket-mad, supporting the Fletching village team, sponsoring nets and hosting dinners after the games. The Griffin also has its own teams, one of which is the Dotties (Dear Old Things) Cricket Club, set up by Nigel in 1998. To join you have to be fifty or over, or 'dotty'. Nigel was captain, James is now, and the team is largely made up of Griffin regulars. They also get involved with the Bonfire Society; all the villages around Lewes have a bonfire in the weeks before November 5th, with a procession and fireworks.

The Griffin is a family business. Says Nigel: "We have lived in the same village, Nutley, three miles from here, for over thirty years now. I had been running restaurants and wine bars and working for large companies. When we bought the pub we thought that our four sons might at some stage need work, and that has duly happened. It has been family-run for the last twenty."

Once a coaching house on the smugglers' route from Newhaven to London it is a very old building, some of it going back six hundred

years. They have done a tremendous amount of work without undermining the rustic mood. The clientele has changed over the years but they have kept the village atmosphere in the sofa-relaxed Club Bar. There are open fires and warm panelling, red carpets and settles, fine prints on the walls.

As for the bedrooms, they are full of little touches and details: complimentary biscotti, locally sourced toiletries. Those in the inn have an uncluttered elegance: uneven floors, soft coloured walls, country furniture, free-standing baths. Each room in the more secluded Coach House has a mural depicting its name: Woolpack, Simon de Montfort, Maypole and Watermill. Swish new rooms in next-door Griffin House are quieter still.

Like all good pub owners, they support their local breweries, of which two are organic: Hepworths and Kings, both of Horsham. Food too is as local as possible, with a large market garden run (organically) by Ian and Nicola Setford half a mile away; suppliers are critically important for James. "We can even say what we would like them to grow for us. We get all our asparagus, peas, squash, salad leaves and flowers from there. They rely on us and we on them.

"We discovered a brilliant fisherman in Rye, Paul Hodges. He now comes five times a week with fresh fish and shellfish, from lobsters to cockles. We have organic veal from a farmer up the road and all the lamb from Romney Marsh."

James went to university in London, worked at the Blue Water Grill in Sydney, then came back to the London bar and restaurant scene.

"The Griffin changed organically but the rot stopped when my brother David came and managed the place. My mother had had live-in managers, which didn't work too well. David came in and made it look good – he then moved on and the buck passed to me. I came down from London fifteen years ago. We grew the kitchen, put bedrooms in the Coach House, did up the garden and bought the house next door. We put in barbecues and won the Best Barbecue in Britain award four years ago. Fish cooking on open drums – food as cabaret!

"I now run the business. It's Slow – we make everything here, even the ice cream and bread. The kitchen is making focaccia bread now. Virtually nothing is bought ready-made.

"There are a lot of good growers and producers round here. They grow for us and we buy everything

they produce. Paul Hodges, the fisherman, was just a man with a boat when we met him. We did a deal with him: everything he landed twice a week we'd buy. Now he supplies all the restaurants round here. There is something about the seashells in Rye Bay; you get a fantastic spectrum of fish.

"Rural businesses need more help from us all. Some people moving to the country from cities

"There is something about the seashells in Rye Bay; you get a fantastic spectrum of fish"

don't use their local shops – they shop in supermarkets, then tear their hair out at the inconvenience when the local shops close.

"You cannot survive solely as a drinking pub – drink-drive legislation has changed all that. Having seven chefs speaks volumes about what we are trying to achieve – and we like running the bar and restaurant menus side by side. People can have a great meal in the restaurant then come round to the bar for a drink to finish the evening. That's how

it works: dyed-in-the-wool Sussex locals may be best friends with the estate owner down the road."

One of James's favourite words is 'scrudging', an invented word to mean "recycling something, and giving it another life". It could be something from a skip or a river, it could be a 600-year-old pub. It is an honourable activity. The combination here of passion with success is powerful, and this Sussex community is enriched by the Pullan family's commitment. The Griffin is, in every respect, an exemplary English pub.

Bridget, Nigel & James Pullan

The Griffin Inn,
Fletching, Uckfield, TN22 3SS
- 13 rooms. £85-£145.
- Singles, midweek, £60-£80.
- Main courses £22-£30; bar meals £10-£20.
- 01825 722890
- www.thegriffininn.co.uk
- Train station: Haywards Heath

Dadmans

KENT

In orchard country is Dadmans, "laden with history but not remotely spooky", once two 16th-century cottages later linked to form one. The bell hanging on the east elevation supports the theory that the house was once a school. Now it is in more elegant hands, surrounded by fields of grazing sheep and cattle, and cherry and apple orchards. As for the curious name, it comes from the Dodmanny family that once lived here.

It has become the sort of house that any glossy magazine would be proud to feature: comfortable, in immensely good taste, full of books and splashes of colour. Bedrooms have patterned fabrics, fresh flowers and good bathrooms, one heavily beamed with a claw-foot bath. Amanda read History of Art while doing up the house yet managed to continue making jams and compotes on her Aga. In the autumn she forages for sloes, and gathers apples for the juice served at breakfast.

Amanda and Pip's parents were neighbours living not far from here. They were unlikely not to get together, and indeed met up later, on a sailing boat off the Cornish coast. Why the B&B? "Pip is retired - a surveyor. We have spare rooms, spare energy, and we enjoy entertaining." They now do everything themselves, gardening and cooking, working on planting schemes including masses of spring bulbs, and breeding interesting species rare breed chickens. But there is no sense of strain: they have bundles of energy and this is what they love.

The Slow aspects come naturally: a refusal to use a microwave or to join the consume-and-discard society, an enjoyment of real food, convivial meals and good company. The bread is homemade. Vegetables and fruit are grown at Dadmans or sourced locally, the meat comes from Mr Doughty who is still licensed to slaughter, and the beef from the neighbouring fields. Fish comes from 'Blue' in Oare or

'Herman's Plaice', and there are excellent farmers' markets in Faversham and Canterbury.

"One of the reasons people come here is because they like the personal touch, to meet the owners and discover how we live and work. We want our guests to feel part of the household but at the same time be waited upon and spoiled. We keep it quite small-scale to keep it fun, treating strangers as friends. And, because this is often the first or last port of call for foreign visitors, we experience a rewarding mix of languages and cultures round the dining table."

Having a fine garden is a great help if you want to be happily Slow. Amanda and Pip have poured energy and imagination into theirs. They bought the house because of the trees, and have planted many more. Kent is widely known as the 'Garden of England' and the soil is perfect for fruit. They have Peasgood

"We keep it quite small-scale to keep it fun, treating strangers as friends"

Nonesuch apples and Morello cherries, walnuts, hazels (grown both for cob nuts and sticks for the garden) and conference pears, blueberries, loganberries and a greenhouse bursting with tomatoes.

Composting is important here; there is an impressive row of compost bins. The vegetable garden is fenced against rabbits and includes wonderful stands of sweet peas. The flowers find their way into the house in summer, casting their fragrance into bedrooms and dining room.

John Keats is generally given credit for first using the name 'sweet pea' in the early 1800s... "Here are sweet peas, on tiptoe for a flight, With wings of gentle flush o'er delicate white."

The hens are all rare breeds; some lay blue eggs, others have fabulous pompoms on their heads.

The country's oldest independent brewer Shepherd Neame is down the road in Faversham; you can smell the sweet barley and malt on the air if you are in town on 'mashing' days. Kent was also England's main

producer of hops for the brewing industry – a few hop fields remain – and Londoners in their thousands would migrate down to the fields for hop-picking work. Perhaps that was in Dicken's mind when he wrote The Pickwick Papers: 'Kent, sir, everyone knows Kent – apples, cherries, hops and women'.

There is an especially rich concentration of things to do and see in Kent. Once the world's first passenger railway line, the Crab and Winkle, ran nearby. It carried oysters from Whitstable to Canterbury; now it is a path for cyclists and walkers. Whitstable's oysters are known as Royal Natives, with exceptionally white shells and a reputation that reached as far as Rome. The Roman historian Salus wrote: 'The poor Britons, there is some good in them after all: they produce an oyster.' Whitstable lives on, loved for its cockle stalls, its fish market and its oysters; there's even a festival held in their honour in July.

You can walk the Saxon Shore Way from Conyer Creek to Faversham, and watch birds (now that is seriously Slow) on the RSPB reserve. You can borrow a bike and follow a cycle route. You can visit Canterbury and re-boot your long-forgotten store of historical memories. A short drive away are Deal, Walmer and Dover castles, all battlements and dark passageways, and Leeds Castle, which has seen more of England's history than most places and is set on two islands in the heart of Kent.

It would be a shame not to taste the local ale. On one of the most charming streets in the country, the Anchor at Faversham, a friendly little place with a big grassy garden at the rear, serving fresh crab and Romney Marsh lamb, and ales from Shepherd Neame.

Amanda Strevens

Dadmans,
Lynsted, Sittingbourne ME9 0JJ
- 2 rooms. £85.
- Dinner £15-£35.
- 01795 521293
- www.dadmans.co.uk
- Train station: Sittingbourne/Faversham

Norfolk   London   Gloucestershire

Herefordshire Worcestershire Shropshire   Derbyshire

ENGLAND: CENTRAL & EAST

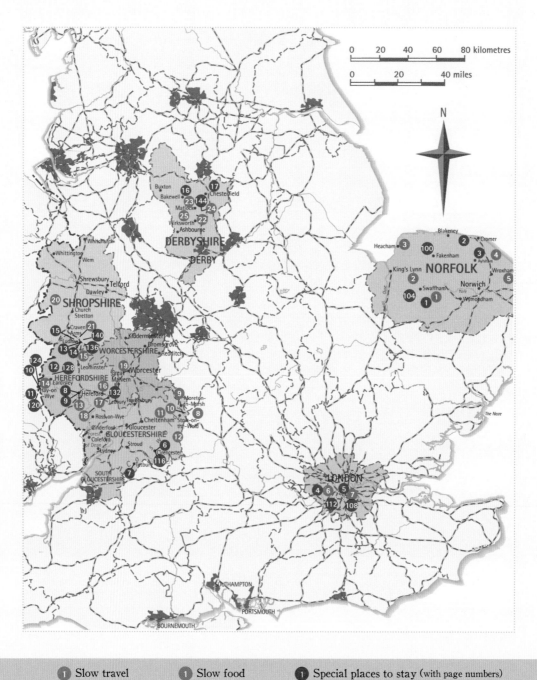

Slow travel   Slow food   Special places to stay (with page numbers)

ENGLAND: CENTRAL & EAST

Slow travel

1. Church of St Mary the Virgin
2. Great Massingham Walk
3. Norfolk Lavender
4. Mundesley
5. Hunter's Yard
6. Petersham Nurseries & Café
7. Horniman Museum
8. Oxfordshire Cycleway
9. Bourton House
10. Chastleton House
11. Cotswold Farm Park
12. Cotswolds Woollen Weavers
13. Mappa Mundi
14. Hay on Wye to the Warren
15. Berrington Hall
16. Green Woodwork Courses
17. Ledbury Cycle Route
18. Hellens
19. Elgar's Birthplace Museum
20. Mitchell's Fold Stone Circle
21. Moral Fibre Felt-making Mill
22. Arkwright Mill
23. Haddon Hall
24. Lea to Dethick Walk
25. National Stone Centre

Slow food

1. Iceni Brewery
2. Cookies Crab Shop
3. Samphire
4. Chelsea Physic Garden
5. Borough Market
6. Abbey Home Farm
7. The Chef's Table
8. Café @ All Saints Church
9. Mousetrap Cheese
10. The Granary
11. River Café
12. Dunkerton Cider Company
13. Deli on the Square
14. De Grey's
15. Ludlow Food Centre
16. Chatsworth Farm Shop
17. Northern Tea Merchants

Special places to stay (with page numbers)

Slow travel

① Church of St Mary the Virgin
Houghton on the Hill
(01760 440470)
Personal guided tours by church warden Bob Davey MBE, devoted to the rescue and revival of this remote hilltop church. It's as loved by visitors as by locals. Remarkable wall paintings go back to Saxon times.

② Great Massingham Walk
Easy-peasy two-hour walk along the long-distance Peddars Way. Begin at the village of Great Massingham, with its four large ponds on four greens; lunch at the lovely Dabbling Duck. Much is open to cyclists, too.
www.walkingworld.com

③ Norfolk Lavender
Heacham (01485 570384)
Lavender farm of over 120 acres with tours and shop. In 1932 three men and a boy did the planting in eighteen days for a total cost of £15. Discover the secrets of distilling.
www.norfolklavender.co.uk

④ Mundesley
Follow the cliff top path for breezes and views of the vibrant beach huts below. When the tide's out there's a sandy beach for safe swimming, tidal pools for toddlers and a beachside café. The lovely Stow Windmill is close by.

⑤ Hunter's Yard
Ludham (01692 678263)
Step back in time on these 1930s gaff sloops: no engines, no noise, just oil lamps, gleaming mahogany and self-tacking jibs. Borrow a skipper for two hours – or two days – and ply the bird-beautiful Norfolk Broads.
www.huntersyard.co.uk

⑥ Petersham Nurseries & Café
Richmond (020 8940 523)
Chef Skye Gingell has elevated a simple café in a plant nursery to a 'fete champêtre' of relaxed rusticity. Surrounded by species roses, rare Chinese peonies, designer wellies - the countryside comes to town.
www.petershamnurseries.com

⑦ Horniman Museum
Forest Hill (020 8699 1872)
Wonderfully eccentric collection of a rich London tea merchant: where else would you find a 1937 jazz drum kit and an old stuffed walrus? Hilltop park boasts rabbits, goats and great views. Entry free.
www.horniman.ac.uk

⑧ Oxfordshire Cycleway
Chipping Norton (01608 642667)
Route 5 of the National Cycle Network runs through Woodstock to Oxford and ends in Banbury. Easyriders organises trips on the third Sunday of the month, with pub lunches: "we don't go too far or too fast".

⑨ Bourton House
Bourton-on-the-Hill
(01386 700754)
Evolving, award-winning gardens, and delicious homemade cakes in the 16th-century tithe barn.
www.bourtonhouse.com

⑩ Chastleton House
Chastleton (01608 674355)
Rare Jacobean house with topiary gardens that, until the early 90s, was lived in continuously for 400 years by one family. No ropes, no barriers, and a kitchen last cleaned in 1612.
www.nationaltrust.org.uk

⑪ Cotswold Farm Park
Guiting Power (01451 850307)
Soay sheep, bristly pigs with striped piglets and other medieval marvels at a special farmyard on Bemborough Farm. Lambing end March to early May, shearing end May to early July, milking from early May, farm safari rides all year.
www.cotswoldfarmpark.co.uk

⑫ Cotswolds Woollen Weavers
Filkins (01367 860491)
The clack of loom-shuttles and the smell of wool oil: wool made the Cotswolds rich. Wonderful 18th-century mill, museum, yarn shop and coffee shop.

13 Mappa Mundi

Hereford Cathedral (01432 374200)
See how 13th-century cartographers perceived the world – the six-foot parchment includes a Norwegian on skis accompanied by a bear!
www.herefordcathedral.org

14 Hay on Wye to the Warren

Walk down the river path by St Mary's Church to this beautiful beach for a barbecue and a swim – with or against the current. Watch the kayaks negotiate the rapids.
www.paddlesandpedals.co.uk

15 Berrington Hall

Near Leominster (01568 615721)
An austere 18th-century exterior hides an interior rich in treasures – plus dairy, laundry, butler's pantry and stables. Park landscaped by Capability Brown.
www.nationaltrust.org.uk

16 Green Woodwork Courses

Bosbury (01531 640125)
Weekend to nine-day courses with Gudrun Leitz, beginning with cleaving wood from a freshly felled tree through to making hedgerow chairs and stools.
www.greenwoodwork.co.uk

17 Ledbury Cycle Route

Ledbury (01531 633433)
See, hear and sniff the countryside, and visit some of the county's cider producers on the twenty-mile

Ledbury route. Cycle hire from Saddlebound.
www.saddleboundcycles.co.uk

18 Hellens

Much Marcle (01531 660504)
Gorgeous, privately owned manor house, open to visitors in summer. Outside: a rare octagonal dovecote, a walled knot garden and an avenue of Hellens Early pears planted in 1710 to commemorate the coronation of Queen Anne.
www.hellensmanor.com

19 Elgar's Birthplace Museum

Lower Broadheath (01905 333 224)
Cottage and museum where manuscripts, music scores, letters, photographs and programmes illustrate the musical life of the creator of 'Land of Hope and Glory'.
www.elgarmuseum.org

20 Mitchell's Fold Stone Circle

Chirbury (01939 232771)
Bronze Age stone circle with dramatic views, once consisting of thirty or more stones, now down to fifteen.
www.english-heritage.org.uk

21 Moral Fibre Felt-making Mill

Stanton Lacy (01584 856654)
The only mill in the country dedicated to the art of felt making, with new wet felting machine in converted barn. Make your own felt slippers.
www.moralfibre.uk.com

22 Arkwright Mill

Cromford (01629 823256)
World Heritage Site celebrating the world's first successful water-powered spinning mill: in 1771 ex-wig maker Arkwright helped launch the Industrial Revolution. Restaurants, shops, events an' all.
www.arkwrightsociety.org.uk

23 Haddon Hall

Bakewell (01629 812 855)
Heavenly house dating from the 1200s, full of uneven flagstones and tapestries, in terraced Elizabethan gardens awash with clematis and old roses.
www.haddonhall.co.uk

24 Lea to Dethick Walk

Starting from Lea, five glorious miles of woodland (bluebells in spring), dell and hill, taking in Dethick's tiny church (1201), a parkful of deer, llama and Cromford Canal.
www.walkingworld.com

25 National Stone Centre

Matlock
(01629 825 403)
Six former quarries, four lime kilns, 120 disused lead mine shafts and a Discovery Centre with quizzes. Trails and dry stone wall courses – good fun.
www.nationalstonecentre.org.uk

Slow food

1 Iceni Brewery
Ickburgh (01842 878922)
Call to arrange a brewery tour;
sniff the malt, rub the hops, taste
the beers.
www.icenibrewery.co.uk

2 Cookies Crab Shop
Salthouse (01263 740352)
Seafood straight from the boats, to
take away or eat in. Lovely to sit
outside and consume your fruits de
mer - pure Norfolk.
www.cookies.shopkeepers.co.uk

3 Samphire
Aylsham (01263 734464)
A treasure in the grounds of
Blickling Hall (National Trust),
run with passion by Nell
Montgomery. Breads, brownies,
smoked mackerel, vegetables in
season, perfect pies laced with
onion marmalade.
www.samphireshop.co.uk

4 Chelsea Physic Garden
(020 7352 5646)
Wondrous al fresco buffet dining
in serene, walled botanists' garden.
The first greenhouse was built
here in 1681. Check opening times.
www.chelseaphysicgarden.co.uk

5 Borough Market
Slow food heaven in Southwark
(south-east of Tate Modern) where
celebrity foodies mix with city
bankers and trendy East Enders.
Open Thurs-Sat.
www.boroughmarket.org.uk

6 Abbey Home Farm
Cirencester (01285 640441)
Farm walks and tractor trailor
tours. Rustic café serves seriously
local food and fab Sunday lunches
with organic meat from the farm;
cheese making courses, and eco
camp too (see p 116).
www.theorganicfarmshop.co.uk

7 The Chef's Table
Tetbury (01666 504466)
In civilised Tetbury, deli, bistro and
cookery school specialising in
simple rustic French dishes from
inspired chef Michael Bedford and
his team.
www.thechefstable.co.uk

8 Café @ All Saints Church
Hereford (01432 370415)
Relying on a network of fantastic
local producers the menu changes
according to the seasons; apple
juices (Katy, Greensleeves, Worcester
Pearmain) come from Jus Apples.

9 Mousetrap Cheese
Hereford (01568 720307)
Quaint little cheese shop two steps
from the cathedral. From Pleck Farm
comes Little Hereford – like
Wensleydale without the tartness.

10 The Granary
Hay on Wye (01497 820790)
Grab-a-table-if-you-can bistro in
England's secondhand bookshop
capital. Beams, dried flowers, winter
fire, outside tables, local beers and
(mostly) veggie/vegan food.

11 River Café
Glasbury Bridge (01497 847007)
Wholesome soups and packed
lunches for a day on the Wye; kayaks
and canoes alongside. Watch the
river from the decking, or a sofa.
www.wyevalleycanoes.co.uk

12 Dunkerton Cider Company
Pembridge (01544 388653)
First organic cider and perry makers
in Herefordshire. Pressed by a 1930s
mill, rare apples include Foxwhelp
(sharp), Kingston Black (bittersharp)
and Court Royal (sweet).

13 Deli on the Square
Ludlow (01584 877353)
Cheeses, mustards, 'Garden' cake
steeped in prunes, figs, walnuts and
damson gin, and Jo Hilditch's crème
de cassis, made with Herefordshire
blackcurrants.
www.delionthesquareludlow.co.uk

14 De Grey's
Ludlow (01584 872764)
An army of waitresses in black
uniforms and starched caps ferry
florentines, tartlettes, eccles
cakes, buns, iced fancies, cream puffs
and moist sponges to well-dressed
tables. www.degreys.co.uk

15 Ludlow Food Centre
Ludlow (01584 856000)
Prolific makers of the Fidget Pie!
Over eighty per cent of food sold
here is locally produced or grown,
and shoppers can stop for a
fairtrade cuppa in the Conservatory
Barn Café. Pretty Ludlow is slow
food capital of Britain.
www.ludlowfoodcentre.co.uk

16 Chatsworth Farm Shop
Pilsley (01246 583392)
One of the first - set up by the
Duchess herself. Creamy lavender
cheese, purple basil pesto, grouse
from Bolton Abbey, and restaurant.
www.chatsworth.org

17 Northern Tea Merchants
Chesterfield (01246 232600)
Purveyors since 1926 of organic
teas and coffees. Quaint shop
delivers tasty, often fairtrade brews
accompanied by cream teas and
cucumber sandwiches.

Pubs & inns

Three Horseshoes

Warham, Norfolk
A former row of cottages a mile from saltmarshes. Three gas-lit rooms with pianola have barely changed since the thirties and the fare is in keeping: locally shot game, hearty casseroles, Wherry straight from the cask. 01328 710547

The Pigs

Edgefield, Norfolk
Homemade pork scratchings, old-fashioned pub games, decent cask ales and real food locally sourced - some of it from the patrons' gardens. No hushed gastro museum this, just a great foodie pub. 01263 587634

Jerusalem Tavern

Clerkenwell, London
Step into a reincarnation of a nooked Georgian interior, candlelit at night with a winter fire; before six you might get a table. St Peter's Brewery have stocked it with their characterful ales, food is simple perfect English. 020 7490 4281

Woolpack Inn

Slad, Gloucestershire
In a lush Cotswolds valley, three little rooms packed with rusticity and charm. Ale from the Uley brewery is as important as the 'nose-to-tail' bar menu: tuck into the simple best. No wonder it heaves at weekends. 01452 813429

Butcher's Arms

Eldersfield, Worcestershire
A two-room pub for Slow Foodies with a big garden and a sensibly short menu: James cooks for just 18 covers at a time. Also a place for popping in for a pint - local beer or cider straight from the cask. All round lovely. 01452 840381

Riverside Inn

Aymestrey, Herefordshire
An easy mix of antiques, flowers, hops and pine. Wander from the bar into linked rooms with log fires for Slow Food that changes with the seasons. The setting is bucolic; the Mortimer Trail passes the front door. 01568 708440

Crown County Inn

Munslow, Shropshire
A sun-trap terrace ouside, dark polished tables and a log-stoved bar within, and walls adored with food awards and a map of suppliers. A treat for lovers of lesser known cheeses including the hop-rolled Hereford Hop. 01584 841205

Mill Race

Walford, Herefordshire
A stainless steel kitchen glistens stylishly behind a .granite bar. The chef chooses the meat and veg from their own farm, the sous-chef catches the trout and kids love the garlic bread. Sip ales from the valley below. Fabulous. 01989 562891

Barley Mow

Kirk Ireton, Derbyshire
It's stone-mullioned and Jacobean, with a sundial dated 1683. Barrels of ale are racked behind the tap room bar, benches line the walls; it's austere, dim-lit and addictive. Lunchtime rolls and trusted ales. 01335 370306

1 Leicester Meadows

NORFOLK

News of Bob and Sara's peaceful idyll, a thirteen-acre collage of woodland and meadows, just a few miles from the North Norfolk coast, seemed to travel fast among the bird community. It wasn't long before a family of geese set up home by the pond, soon joined by a covert of coots and the occasional heron; then came a guinea fowl who adopted the couple's small brood of Maram hens; in late Spring, Greylag geese drop by for an extended vacation. A particularly bold green woodpecker likes to strut outside the dining room windows, partridges and pheasants play catch over the meadows, barn and tawny owls hoot haunting solos in the woods, while buzzards and marsh harriers keep silent watch overhead.

From the house, views drift over softly rolling hills and fields, the grass-green tones spliced by bright yellow slivers of rapeseed and shimmering blue linseed. Animals scurry among the trees, meadows are traced by winding, mown paths, the River Burn trickles past and lawns spill gently down through layers of terraces. There is not another building in sight and the peace is absolute.

The old farm workers' cottages, of brick and flint, once part of the Holkham Estate owned by the Earls of Leicester, were utterly derelict when Bob and Sara first arrived, having moved just a quarter of a mile from the farmhouse in which

their three children grew up. "First we planted a vegetable garden and built a chicken run. Only then did we tackle the cottages," says Bob. "We got our priorities straight."

The couple are now twelve years into a twenty-year renovation project that has seen the two cottages spliced into one large house with a barn next door, and a long, winding driveway flanked by a parade of young chestnuts. Underfloor heating is powered by an air-to-water heat pump and they are considering the installation of photovoltaic cells on a rear roof.

"No doubt when we have done all the work we'll come up with another twenty-year plan," says Bob, whose many years of professional experience as an architect specialising in rescuing old, redundant buildings has been instrumental in the transformation of the house. Sara, who trained as a furniture designer and specialised in teaching three-dimensional art and textiles, has a penchant for collecting, including art, furniture and beautiful, often quirky porcelain. These complimentary skills have produced a simple, unpretentious and peaceful place to stay. The emphasis is on "quality of life not materialism" so don't expect gadgets or gizmos. Sara insists on getting the important things right and on making the little gestures

that show they care. Rooms are spotless, with ironed sheets and vases of fresh flowers, while breakfasts, served on pale blue Poole pottery in the lovely kitchen and dining room, are generous, with homemade breads and jams, locally-sourced rare breed sausages and bacon, and eggs laid by the Maram hens. In the garden you can find tomatoes, lettuces, potatoes and courgettes; nearby are apple and quince trees and bushes bursting with berries. They make their own cordial by raiding local hedgerows, and grape juice from a vine clinging to the south side of the house.

Bob and Sara share a horror of letting worthwhile things go to waste so you'll find that everything in the house has a story, from the 'vintage' pub sign in the entrance hall (rescued from a film set) to the oak staircase, saved from a town-centre warehouse. Beautiful, shapely brick fireplaces house large wood-burners and the old bread oven is now a feature of Bob's study. Revitalising old things is a lifelong passion for the couple.

Bob and Sara are generous with their time. "We spend time with guests who wish to chat, but give space and privacy to those who just want to unwind," says Bob. And you should certainly give yourselves the time to explore this gentle county of Norfolk, whose fertile fields of wheat and barley are punctuated by villages and stately homes, a coastline of bird reserves, boats and sandy beaches. Archaeological sites testify to centuries of rich history: the Iron Age hill fort of Bloodgate Hill is a pleasant walk away and the village church, with its great angel roof containing lead shot ascribed to Cromwell's troops. Walking and cycling are popular, with many green lanes stretching uninterrupted for miles. Bob, however, is eager to dispel Noel Coward's assertion that Norfolk is 'very flat'.

Although the family has lived near South Creake, a quiet community of five-hundred people, a pub, church and village green, for over twenty years, it wasn't until relatively recently, after Sara had been involved in the preparation of the Village Plan and Bob had taken over production of the Creake News,

that they became aware of artists, writers and fascinating people living here. "We never cease to be amazed – even after such a long time."

Bob, Sara and friends have initiated a 'Virtual Village Hall' – in the form of a village picnic and other community events – after the old village hall was forced to close. South Creake and nearby North Creake have an active music and arts scene, too. The North Norfolk Music Festival takes place every September and the Yorke Trust, which is involved with the training of young musicians, holds regular concerts throughout the year.

Bob and Sara are open-minded about the future but insist on several, laudable principles: that the peace must be preserved, that we must be more responsible with the earth's resources, and that quality of life takes precedence. "We'll have a few more adventures yet," says Bob.

Sara & Bob Freakley

1 Leicester Meadows,
South Creake, Fakenham, NR21 9NZ
- 2 rooms.
- £65-£75.
- Dinner occasionally available, from £20.
- 01328 823533
- www.leicestermeadows.com
- Train station: King's Lynn

Strattons

NORFOLK

Strattons is about as Slow as can be, combining a profound belief in the value of slow living with passionately held ecological practice. If a prize were awarded to the British hotel with the smallest ecological footprint per guest, then Strattons would probably win it.

They weigh their total business and domestic waste and harvest 200,000 litres of waste water each year for re-use; the salad crops are one beneficiary. Twenty years ago they wrote their first environmental policy and have rewritten it every year. They also have a special recycling room where they sort magazines for the old people's home, the doctors' waiting rooms and the library; newspapers make firebricks or are shredded for animal bedding; wax is used to make new candles. The staff are steeped in it and the hotel has won numerous awards.

A creative zest is at work at Strattons. Les and Vanessa support other local businesses and positively encourage local artists, putting money back into the community to keep it alive. Their latest enterprise, completed in 2010, is the restoration of the old print workshop on the south boundary, a workshop run by several generations of the Coe family. Space has been created for two new bedrooms and self-catering suites – and CoCoes, a sparkling new café deli. Building on her long-standing relationships with local producers

and growers, Vanessa is able to offer heathery honeys, succulent terrines and superb Norfolk cheeses from makers Jane Murray, Ellie Betts and Catherine Temple. Take your spoils home or sit down and tuck in. Served with homemade crackers and damson paste, washed down with an organic or bio-dynamic wine, a platter of CoCoes cheeses is one of life's pleasures.

Shutters keep the winter heat in, light bulbs are mostly low energy and the newest rooms have a master switch that shuts down all the lights and devices at once. Miniature toiletry bottles have been replaced with liquid dispensers, soaps are made (organically) by a Norwich soapmaker. The list of housekeeping commitments goes on, and spills outside, to bat boxes, bird boxes and ponds in the wildlife garden. Inside, the beautiful, graceful mermaid mosaic running along the back of the bath in the Portico Room is made from kitchen waste, including seashells and broken crockery.

Another challenge, of course, is to run the hotel with fun and originality. Being 'chic' is harder, but for Les and Vanessa, who met at art college, a stylish mix of old and new comes naturally. There's a touch of panache in every corner and the rooms are constantly reinventing themselves. The Venetian Room has a high old Italian style bed, zebra-print rugs and silver globe lights.

The bathroom is tiled in black slate, the mirror is Venetian, and the view is over the green and secluded garden, dotted with free-range bantams, beautified by recycled metal sculptures, tables and chairs. The Seagull Room creates yet a different mood, all sea and sand colours, with slatted wooden blinds and a faux-fur bedspread. The Opium Suite is in a separate building across the lawn with a big double bath at the foot of the bed so that you can fall, blissfully, from one into the other. All rooms have wind-up radios, all have a book full of cycle routes and walks, and there's a 10% discount for those arriving by bus or train.

The Brecks is the name for this distinctive inland region. A landscape of sheep walks, medieval rabbit warren and temporary fields known as 'Brecks' which has been allowed to revert back to heath abounding with wildlife: red deer, roe deer, muntjaks and hares.

> "Les and his team talk you through the cheeseboard with panache, and organic breakfast is scrumptious"

Thetford Forest, which spreads itself across eighty square miles, is the largest lowland pine forest in Britain. Started in the 1920s as a strategic timber reserve, it is now home to red squirrels, woodlarks and nightjars. You can drive into it, ride through it on cycle or horseback, even scale the forest canopy with an aerial trekking facility. The most characteristic symbols of this countryside are the hedges and shelter belts of Scots pines planted as windbreaks at the time of Enclosure, from 1768 onwards, to stop the precious topsoil (for the farming of turf) from blowing away. They line the roads and edges of the fields, their branches and trunks twisted by age and the elements – very striking.

Swaffham is an interesting Regency town. County families would go there for the season and so too would the clergy. When berated by the Bishop who thought they should stay in their parishes, they would reply that they could perfectly well see their parishes from the high ground of Swaffham.

Strattons itself is an interesting building. It probably began as a malting barn then became a villa in the eighteenth century, with a couple of added wings. Perhaps it was a sort of Palladian weekend retreat for a Norwich family; many such villas were built within close reach of the busy cities. The Scotts bought it in 1990 and had to rip out the nylon carpets and woodchip wallpaper. "It was like a beautiful old lady over whose face someone had smeared too much lipstick." They had always loved doing up old houses and one day, after a dinner party in their last house, someone frivolously suggested that they charge people for coming. So they looked for somewhere larger for just that.

Vanessa grew up in a large household with hordes of visiting friends, two grandmothers and a mother who were great cooks, always baking and making country food. "I was always welcome to bring friends home and my mother was never fazed by putting meals together."

Here, in the candlelit restaurant, the food is mostly local and organic where possible – nettle and barley broth, slow-cooked leg of Papworth lamb, rhubarb and ginger crème brûlée. Les and his team talk you through the cheeseboard with panache, and organic breakfast is scrumptious.

Vanessa & Les Scott

Strattons
4 Ash Close, Swaffham, PE37 7NH
- 10 rooms. £150-£175. Singles from £120. Suites from £200.
- Dinner, 4 courses £40.
- 01760 723845
- www.strattonshotel.com
- Train station: Downham Market or King's Lynn

24 Fox Hill

LONDON

Frogs sing, owls hoot at night, squirrels scamper, woodpeckers wake you in the morning, and central London is twenty minutes away by train.

Fox Hill is a leafy oasis in South London, a red-brick 1880s semi-detached house, an unusual and inspiring place to stay when visiting the capital. The views from the top of the road are huge, reaching to the Home Counties on a fine day; the air is clear, the skies are open, and there's a garden too, bigger and more peaceful than most city gardens, with a shady, jasmine-scented terrace and a raised pond with lilies and goldfish and gurgling water. It is long and lush with tree ferns and exotic acers and arums, and a coop full of predator-protected hens. Foxes have their own way of dividing modern urban communities; some people feed them, chicken fanciers hate them. Sue and Tim have a sneaking admiration for them, expressed in the fox-shaped brass door knocker on the front door.

Sue has a deep-rooted conviviality that was nurtured by a nomadic childhood with a Navy father who met her Canadian mother during the war. She was hauled from one country to another, attending thirteen schools and meeting people from every corner of the world.

"I like a rich diet of people and I absolutely love doing B&B. Given

a little time here, most people fold into the life of the family. Teachers, doctors, Nobel prize-winners, Japanese TV stars, Christian publishers from South Korea – we never know who will next come through the door! Of everyone who comes I think, 'there is going to be something delicious about you, and I am going to find it'. We live in a sort of human advent calendar; it's wonderful."

That heart-warming expression of warmth speaks volumes about staying here, and reflects the sentiment of Hebrews: 'Be not forgetful to entertain strangers: for thereby some have entertained angels unawares.'

The house throbs with family atmosphere and vitality (aided by Shreddie the dog and Hudson the cat) and Sue and Tim's dinners (produce from the garden, eggs from the hens) are convivial occasions – great fun. Tim too was brought up in many different countries. His father was a military scientist, part of the team that invented radar. Tim has inherited his energy and after a career in IT now works with the Depaul Trust that rescues children from the streets; the projects cover the UK, Eastern Europe and the USA. He travels a lot, and makes the cooked breakfasts when at home.

There's good stuff everywhere – things hang off walls and peep over the tops of dressers. The

house's big rooms are stuffed with treasures from around the world, and Sue's art. "We both love technology, but my creative side is Slow."

Sue started quilting quite late in life, once the children had flown. The quilts are beautiful, influenced by her stay in America but mainly the product of time spent at Chelsea Art College. She quilts by hand and by machine, doing commissions and presents for friends. When Sue makes a quilt it can take her three years. "I tell Tim that my quilt could last for over 200 years while his computer may last for a mere three!"

All the beds have classic quilts on them and the bedrooms – two big double rooms, and a twin in the eaves – are both colourful and delightful. The stairway is perfect for hanging textiles as there is little light to fade them; Sue hangs some of her best works there, including an exquisite hand-sewn silk work from her end-of-degree show. She is interested in colours, the patterns in plants, felt (which she also makes), dyes and batik. You can see it all here, some with a Latin American influence, others African or Indian (her father was born in India). It gives the house a rare vitality.

Sue leads the family in its search for a slower life. The things she loves doing take time: cooking, gardening, painting, textiles – and foraging for wood for the sitting room's fabulous Swedish stove. With quilts that take up to three years to make, and

"Frogs sing, owls hoot, and central London is twenty minutes by train"

garden plants that take time to grow, there is little point in hurrying. She makes her own bread and jams and is getting to grips with composting and recycling. Sue happily admits that there is much more they could do but they are well on the way; nor do they need any convincing that focussing on life's simple pleasures – nurturing garden and hens, making time for friends old and new – is deeply rewarding.

"What a place to plunder!" said Marshall Blucher, the Prussian General at Waterloo, as he gazed upon London. 'Upper Norwood and Crystal Palace. Exceptionally healthy because of prevailing

wind from the coast – 380 feet above Thames therefore out of valley fogs', says the poster from the Twenties that hangs in the front bathroom. The refreshing winds still prevail today.

Crystal Palace Park is seven minutes' walk away, humming with activity – athletics, concerts, conferences – and home to a Grade I-listed monument and national treasure: the dinosaurs. These sculptures were commissioned in 1852 for the opening of the Park, a Victorian theme park of two hundred acres which received the reconstructed Crystal Palace. It burned down in 1936, but the dinosaurs lived on. They caused a national sensation when unveiled; now two million visitors come to see them every year. Plans are also afoot to turn the park into one of the most spectacular green spaces in Europe.

Trains to Victoria are frequent, the No 3 bus to Oxford Circus is a sightseeing trip in its own right and, thanks to the impending Olympics, Crystal Palace is on the East London line.

From one of the windows one used to be able to see the tree Pissarro painted in 1870; sadly it came down in 2007. Both he and Emile Zola took refuge here from France during the war with Prussia; Pissarro returned in 1871, to discover that only forty of the 1,500 canvasses he had stored there remained. One of a dozen of Pissarro's paintings to survive from this period hangs in the National Portrait Gallery: 'Fox Hill at Norwood'. The National Gallery may be a short train ride away but Crystal Palace is rich in restaurants and museums, too: the country's oldest public gallery, the eccentric Horniman Museum, is close, as is the Dulwich Picture Gallery, the first purpose-built art gallery in the country. Full of Canalettos, Rembrandts, Watteaux and Gainsboroughs, it's a gem.

Sue & Tim Haigh

24 Fox Hill,
Crystal Palace, SE19 2XE
- 3 rooms. £90-£120. Singles £50.
- Dinner £35.
- 020 8768 0059
- www.foxhill-bandb.co.uk
- Train station: Crystal Palace

The Victoria

LONDON

"Good food should not be taken for granted by some yet only aspired to by those on lower incomes. It should be appreciated by everyone and everyone should, and can, eat well," says chef Paul Merrett.

Paul, co-owner of The Victoria, is no stranger to fine dining and his food won Michelin stars at two previous restaurants. In the conservatory dining room at The Victoria, an attractive red-brick pub on a leafy residential street beside Richmond Park, couples and families savour Jersey rock oysters, nettle soup, rabbit cônfit with cranberries and celeriac rémoulade, roast breast of duck with shallot purée and truffle jus.

"In Britain a food revolution is taking place: farmers' markets, organic food shops, farmshops. I'm immensely proud. But behind kitchen doors I feel people are wasting food, not shopping strategically and, as a result, over-spending. One can live very reasonably by shopping carefully, planning meals and using every last bit of food. A roast dinner, for instance, isn't one meal but several: sandwiches, bubble and squeak, broth for a soup. It was obvious to our grandparents, but increasingly forgotten in today's society where ready-prepared fast-food is everywhere." In Paul's television show, the BBC's Economy Gastronomy that he presented with chef Allegra McEvedy, he

encouraged us to eschew take-aways and frozen meals in favour of basic ingredients, bought sensibly and combined simply and well. "The idea was to bring the skills and knowledge of a working chef to the home," says Paul.

When Paul is not facing the cameras he is pouring his abundant energy into the food at The Victoria, while his co-owner Greg Bellamy takes care of front of house. A New Zealander who arrived in London for the Rugby World Cup of '91 and never went home, Greg's style of service is attentive and professional yet relaxed. "Diners are never hurried and there's almost a holiday feel," he says.

A five-minute stroll from Richmond Park and Sheen Common, the Victoria's location is perfect and is arguably the best 'country' experience you'll get in London yet it's an easy twenty-minute train journey to Waterloo. "We have sports fans who come for Wimbledon and Twickenham and businesspeople who work in Barnes, Putney and Richmond," explains Greg. "Many guests stay for the Hampton Court Flower Show or outdoor concerts at Kew. In the mornings, it's mums and breakfast meetings. It buzzes non-stop." Seven uncluttered bedrooms in an adjoining wing allow those who don't need to dash a lovely space to relax and a stylish launchpad for all that south west London can offer.

The Victoria has a stunning range of wines, all meticulously researched and described with passion and humour by Greg. "Thalassitis from Santorini in Greece, made by the 'George Clooney of wine; like sucking on a frosty volcano'; Australian Ad Hoc Hen & Chicken chardonnay with a sexy hazelnut toastiness; English sparkling – a dazzling fizz with awards a-plenty." The list, originally chosen by wine expert Olly Smith is tweaked and perfected by Greg, whose love and knowledge of wine was sparked by working on his family's New Zealand wine estate.

Paul is passionate about sourcing good quality ingredients, and his sourcing is impeccable. "Our beef comes from a small butcher in Devon," says Paul. "He

> "I had happy memories of helping my grandparents on their allotment, and wanted my kids to have the same experiences"

chooses the cows for us and we've been to the abattoir, too, to check how the animals are treated. I like building up that kind of relationship, it's invaluable." At large markets like Billingsgate or Covent Garden, and at supermarkets, you are removed from the ingredients you are buying and the people who produce them. "I like to deal with butchers, fishermen and farmers who understand their animals and who value good food."

Most fish comes from harbourside markets in Brixham and Falmouth and mussels are from the Norfolk coast. Bread is made fresh daily on the premises using organic flour from Claybrooke mill, a three-hundred-year-old water mill in Leicestershire, and Paul even employs a professional forager for mushrooms, elderflower, seaweed and nettles. He has a close relationship with a small farm in Guildford that grows tomatoes, among other things, for him.

An obsession with ingredients led Paul, in 2007, to attempt a foodie experiment around how we source our food. 'Using The Plot' describes his

family's attempt to survive for a year on produce from their fledgling urban allotment, and includes recipes designed to make the most of seasonal home-grown greens, like One Pot Vegetable Stew and Tea-Smoked Chicken on Allotment Vegetables. It's wry and funny and dissects romantic ideas of cutting entirely our reliance on supermarkets.

"My children grew up as London kids with no idea of where food came from, no clue about the seasons or why they shouldn't waste food," explains Paul. "I had happy memories of time spent helping my grandparents on their allotment, and wanted my kids to have the same experiences. In terms of self-sufficiency we failed miserably: our allotment was raided by squirrels, foxes, magpies, local kids and I put my back out lots of times. It was a sobering experience and made us value good food even more."

Paul and Greg are great running mates for championing the joys of good food cooked well. Together they have created a convivial space imbued with their energy and, most of all, their sense of fun.

Paul Merrett & Greg Bellamy

The Victoria, 10 West Temple Sheen,
Richmond, London, SW14 7RT
- 7: 5 doubles, 2 twins/doubles.
- £115. Singles £105.
- Main courses £10-£18; bar meals £5-£10.
- 020 8876 4238
- www.thevictoria.net
- Train station: Mortlake or Richmond

Abbey Home Farm

GLOUCESTERSHIRE

Hilary doesn't own a car. If necessary, she borrows her husband Will's pickup. "I walk to work most mornings, a mile along the most beautiful old railway line. I don't see anyone else, just cows and sheep and deer and rabbits. It's one of the very best moments of my day." That day will be a busy one, as usual. Hilary runs a separate business within the whole Abbey Home Farm all-organic operation. It embraces the thriving ten-acre vegetable garden, the organic farm shop ("one of the only 100%-certified organic shops I know"), the Verandah Café, the Green Room conference and workshop centre, the Lower Wiggold self-catering cottage and the rustic woodland camping and yurt sites (cold-water tap, outside kitchen, compost loo). Ever the pioneers, they've had a yurt for thirteen years, with a magical walk to the café. "I started with an honesty-box shop and have extended it four times in eleven years. When I have an idea I want to make it happen right away. I'm a jack-of-all-trades, really. I look after the customers, the staff, – there are thirty people here while the farm proper runs with just five employees –, the stock, the light bulbs... with my daughter Bex's help and together we make sure our operations are as organic and ethical as they can possibly be today, knowing there's always room for improvement. My 'help needed'

ad says 'duties include smiling, helping customers, washing up,...'"

The estate is old and Will runs a farm of over six hundred hectares that has been in his family for five hundred years. The story? In 1564 Doctor Richard Master, physician to Elizabeth 1, bought the site of the dissolved monastery and much of its land from the Queen. She presented him with a silver gilt chalice that belonged to her mother Anne Boleyn – which the family gifted to the parish church in the 1960's.

For twenty years, Will and Hilary, both vegetarians, spent long periods in India, learning to appreciate a less consumerist culture and starting a block-printing workshop in Rajasthan to produce fairtrade organic textiles based on old Indian patterns. They lived on the farm and had a shop in Cirencester selling fabrics, old Indian furniture and folk art (now sold in the farm shop). Meanwhile, the farm was run conventionally by Will's grandmother. When Hilary and Will said the farm thought it should 'go organic', the family's answer was always no. Eventually, with three children and too much chemical fertiliser in the air, they were about to move to Devon. "We thought we'd ask one last time – and they said yes!"

Neither is a hands-on farmer but they run it all with informed passion. "We aim to put the earth in good heart, to live and let live, using only nature and our own skills (slugs can take a thousand lettuces in a night...)." Founder members of the Organic Milk Suppliers Cooperative, when conversion was achieved in 1994 they had a hundred Friesian milkers and sold their first product to Yeo Valley. But they weren't convinced that the dairy system of blending milk from all sources fitted their ideals of organic production and traceability. So they now have just twelve Shorthorns for on-farm dairy produce and make their own yoghurt, cheese and butter for café and shop. "My passion is organic food and I believe a farm should provide the local community with ingredients for complete meals, not just one crop that's carried all over the country – or the world. Ideally, nothing comes in and nothing goes out, nothing breaks the circle. That's my aim, that's why we grow beef and pork, lamb and chicken, as well as soft fruit and every

> "My passion is organic food and I believe a farm should provide the local community with ingredients for complete meals, not just one crop that's carried all over the country"

vegetable we can in season. Then there's our honey, dairy produce, and cut flowers too. Our bread is made with our own wheat, our frozen meals inspired by farm produce."

Having seen life, death and famine during her two youthful years in Kenya, Hilary can't bear to see food wasted. She constantly checks the racks for wilting leaves or tired carrots and redirects them towards soup or chutney or pigs. "Our lunches are unbelievably Slow: rich-tasting vegetarian soups, salads mixed for colour and taste using luminous ingredients picked that morning and eaten on the veranda, watching tomorrow's lunch grow in the garden. These salads are famous, they sing with

vitality. On Sundays, the only day we serve meat, we offer one traditional roast beef or pork meal and two vegetarian options."

"The thing I am most proud of, however, is helping to create the Soil Association apprenticeship scheme. A hundred years ago there were twenty work horses here and a stable boy's day was 5am to 7pm. That's unthinkable nowadays but this country sorely lacks skilled growers and you can't learn the job in a classroom, so I and a couple of others pushed and pulled, hassled and argued, and got the idea accepted. Apprentices stay for two years and work in the vegetable garden for minimum wage and a lot of mentoring. There are also a number of formal training modules. They are all so eager to learn, we love having them. We had one of the very first apprentices here three years ago and she has just started a box scheme in Ireland. I feel it's a triumph."

"Our future plans? To keep trying to persuade small Indian cotton growers to go organic, despite Monsanto's sly seduction method of showing farmers videos of gold-bedecked, nail-varnished women and suggesting they will soon be able to give their wives such things – if only they will sign on. To get local authorities here to recognise that windmills are more elegant than pylons and should be encouraged, even in 'places of outstanding natural beauty': I really want to 'green' our electricity consumption, even though the shop, café, office and Green Room are heated with a farm-fed wood-chip boiler. To show people that there is another way."

Hilary Chester-Master

Lower Wiggold at Abbey Home Farm,
Burford Road, Cirencester, GL7 5EZ
- 2 rooms. £600 p.w. Short breaks available.
  Camping from £4 per night.
- Meals in café from £6.50.
- 01285 640441
- www.theorganicfarmshop.co.uk
- Train station: Kemble

Ty-Mynydd

HEREFORDSHIRE

John and Niki have taken with passion to this remote mountainside place, strewn with grazing sheep and raw, green views. Up here, you feel you are on top of the world. These are the Black Hills, brought to us by Bruce Chatwin in his novel On the Black Hill – a bleak tale of two brothers on an isolated farm. The Victorian vicar, Francis Kilvert, whose diaries have become worldwide classics, also walked these hills and coaxed them into the affections of millions. But they remain largely empty, a demanding yet beautiful corner of Britain where England and Wales meet in gentle amity.

John took to building walls and damning streams with stones when he was just eight; his brother, a carpenter, gave him twenty yards of stonewall to build when he was fourteen. That was it; he left school to build dry stone walls. The walling soon led him to farms that needed him, then to buying and doing up houses and selling them on, then, finally, to Ty-Mynydd.

"I had a hankering to run my own farm," he says, and he has done ever since.

He lived on his own up here, busy, active, outdoors in all weathers, content... but alone. So he sent his photograph in to Country Living magazine's The Farmer Wants a Wife campaign. About seventy candidates replied; Niki's letter, declaring that she would be quite happy sitting in front of a fire with a

glass of wine ("mind you, we've never done it!") won him over.

Niki wrote a letter to us about this book; it says more about their lives than we could.

"Our lives, along with our organic farm and B&B here in the Black Mountains, run along 'slow' principles. Our animals graze freely (cows, goats, geese, sheep and Oxford Sandy and Black pigs) over acres of ancient organic pastureland, with hardly any human intervention. They live and grow at their own natural pace, calving and lambing where they choose. Being organic, they are fed no artificial foodstuffs at all. When the time comes to slaughter, the animals undergo a thirty-minute drive (minimum stress) to a local abattoir/butchers.

"Our meat is then hung and matured for a month and believe me, it is worth the wait. Our eggs are supplied by my chickens, so B&B guests, at breakfast, get to sample produce born and raised on the fields they view from their window."

The farm is a joint effort between Niki and John. Stonemasonery is still his first trade, and he is sympathetically restoring a seventeenth-century farmhouse in the historic Llanthony valley nearby. John's dry stone walling can be seen around the farm; keen to pass on the craft, he runs occasional weekend courses.

"People come mainly from London and Bristol to chill out and get back in touch with the rhythms of nature and it is so lovely to get feedback from our guests, especially the ones with young children who have run wild, safe and free. That tells us that we are successfully sharing our way of life with others; what more do you really need? Good fresh local food, healthy clean mountain air and lots of space."

"Add unspoilt views and stunning sunsets and you have the perfect life"

These one hundred and thirty acres of unspoilt pasture and woods with the Blaendigeddi brook running through are free for guests to explore. Follow the bridleway, once an old road, through the land and down the valley into the village of Llanigon, and, if you are feeling fit, on to Hay on Wye. In Hay (six miles as the crow flies) are pubs, restaurants, cafes and second hand bookshops by the score. And in May and June Hay hosts the celebrated Festival of Literature & Arts, described by Bill Clinton, memorably, as "the Woodstock of the mind".

It was Niki who wanted to do it all organically, in spite of organic farming being a relatively unusual concept at the time. Breakfasts here are delicious and the only item that has to travel to the table is the milk; bread is homemade, by hand not machine. The water is from their own spring and tastes as only spring water can. Niki keeps bees – taste the honey! – and the vegetable patch up the hill, bursting with wholesome stuff, often gets invaded by fat hens – not so much free range as all over the place.

She and John are also involved in two agri-environmental schemes (Tir Gofal and Better Woodlands for Wales) which enables them to rejuvenate old hedgerows and fence off an ancient bluebell wood from the grazing animals, something that hasn't been done for nearly a century. Now beautiful carpets of bluebells appear every spring.

"People are fascinated by our lifestyle, and sit and stare out of the window at breakfast time – not

talking, just winding down and taking it all in." At night, Niki lights candles in the windows and by the door so you can find your way in; but linger a while to watch the bats. You'll sleep well – the only sound is sheep – in two sweetly restful bedrooms on the ground floor, with proper eiderdowns, a country bathroom and green views.

It is not always easy, especially in winter, and there's no extra money for holidays. But they feel that the faster the world gets, the slower they want to go; it is so much more enriching and fulfilling. And it is a life only dreamt about when as a lass from the industrial North East, armed with an English degree and all her belongings crammed into a Nissan Micra, Niki turned up at this Welsh mountain farm on a freezing March day.

That is the sort of energy and enthusiasm that changes lives – and places. At the end of the long, bumpy track, the once-dull bungalow, cheaply built and with aluminium windows and hardboard doors, has been transformed by John's vision. When he first came here, there was little birdsong. Now the farm is filled with it, house martins swooping over the fields and into the nests under the eaves. The collies are real characters, including the unstoppable Floss with only three legs. The children, Daniel, eight, and Madeline, six, are sweet-natured and at home in the winter mud and muck.

Altogether, the family and their farm are enough to persuade the most hardened urbanites out of their rural 'denial'. John and Niki are the architects of their own lives; it may be hard work but they avoid much that overwhelms the rest of us.

Niki Spenceley

Ty-Mynydd,
Llanigon, Hay-on-Wye, HR3 5RJ
- 2 rooms.
- From £80. Singles £60.
- 01497 821593
- www.tymynydd.co.uk
- Train station: Hereford

The Peren

HEREFORDSHIRE

Perhaps it was in the Daintree Rainforest in Queensland, Australia, that Simon and Andrew were first bitten with inspiration for The Peren. Or maybe the idea took shape on the dramatic fjords of New Zealand's South Island or while trekking to spot koala bears, king parrots, whales and albatrosses. For it was during a two-month natural history tour through Australia and New Zealand in 2004 – by foot, bus and train – that the Londoners discovered the joy of staying in rural self-catering places that were "full of light, modern, stylish, spotlessly clean and fantastically well-designed". With the Blue Mountains as a backdrop, their imaginations travelled ten thousand miles across the globe to a cottage and smallholding, a thumb-length on the map from Hay-on-Wye in deepest Herefordshire, and a severely dilapidated barn just holding its own in a flower-strewn meadow.

Fast-forward a few years. The wildflower meadow is still there, now dotted with fruit trees and picnic spots amid wide mowed paths. The barn is transformed and magnificent: soaring double-height windows gleam in place of the old threshing doors, floor tiles glow in a waterfall of light cascading through vast French windows. The open-plan design imparts an incredible sense of space, light and clarity. You float upstairs to oak floors, two calm, uncluttered

bedrooms and a lush bathroom sporting stone tiles and a double-ended bath. A glass walkway joins the master bedroom and bathroom – not so much for the extra light, Andrew admits, as for the feeling of fun you get from scampering over the glass.

The abundance of glass in The Peren's design, jigsaw-puzzled among scrubbed stone and neat wood, allows the outside to flood in. And how glorious it is. Your nearest neighbours in front are quietly cropping horses; to the rear lies that wonderful meadow. Beyond is Simon and Andrew's five-acre, organically managed smallholding and the fruits of their labour: courgettes, potatoes, brassicas galore, every imaginable type of bean; a poly-tunnel for salads; an orchard of pears, damsons, greengages, a young mulberry bush. Guests get whatever's in season, along with eggs from a small flock of chickens. Sheep and pigs also play their part; Andrew is learning to cure the pork and make sausages.

The copious wildlife and birdlife around The Peren – otters, badgers, red kites, buzzards, owls, merlins, green and lesser-spotted woodpeckers – is down to the stocked bird-feeders, chemical-free soil and some good research and experimentation. A recently planted patch of teasel has attracted the latest newcomers, a contented family of goldfinches.

Tempting as it is to stay within this miniature natural paradise, you're encouraged to venture out and work your way gradually through Simon and Andrew's 'Top Five' lists. Among these, the magical Llanthony Priory in the heart of the Black Mountains, canoeing on the River Wye and horse-riding on the area's quiet, rural trails rate highest with most guests. The Wye Valley Walk and Herefordshire Trail ramble off into the distance. You can throw your car keys into the bottom of your suitcase for the duration. A local company delivers and collects bicycles, with a discount for guests. Hay-on-Wye, with its farmers' market, independent shops and second-hand bookstores, is a flat mile-and-a-half meander away.

'Peren' is Welsh for pear. This was previously a plantation of perry trees – small, acidic pears pressed for perry cider – in what is still a cider-producing area. Historians can dig deep into the history of this agricultural land. For centuries Clifford, wrapped in a fold of the River Wye between a 'cliff' and a 'ford', teetering dangerously on the Welsh border, was the victim of fierce land ownership battles between England and Wales. Now it's a charming, scattered hamlet with thirty houses, an active community and the ruins of a once-great castle.

Despite the sense of nature that surrounds you, there's more than a whiff of 'eco-chic'. "There was a time when 'eco' or 'environmental' conjured up images of big woolly jumpers and sandals," says Andrew, "but that's not what we're about."

Since their escape from London, Simon and Andrew have shown that it is possible to combine modern work life with the principles of Slow living. Andrew, a high-level charity fundraiser, acts as an independent consultant for clients such as the Landmark Trust and the Rose Theatre on London's South Bank. Simon's career is in public relations and media consultancy for environmental organisations, including the National Trust and WWF. In between planting seeds and pulling on hiking boots, he helps promote the Goldman Environmental Prize, billed as the Oscars of the environmental world. He also turns his expertise to helping Hay become a 'transition

town' – gearing itself up to switch from oil-based energy supplies to local, sustainable sources.

At The Peren underfloor heating is powered by geothermal energy from a ground source heat pump, and the sitting room's Swedish log-burning stove burns wood from their own sustainable plantation of ash trees. FSC-certified wood, salvaged tiles, reclaimed timber and low-energy lighting also work towards making the barn conversion ecologically sound. And while everything is high-spec, there are delicate touches of the down-to-earth and local: the little antique kitchen table, for instance, was picked up for five-pounds at a nearby auction.

It is ironic that The Peren's story started in the exotic landscapes of Australia, because the overriding theme is of local goods and local people. When Andrew set up a monthly farmer's market in Clifford, he discovered the wealth of resources and talents hidden in Herefordshire's seemingly sleepy villages. "I was staggered at the number of high quality producers and craftspeople," he says. Here you will find wrought-iron stair rails cast locally; curtains sewn by a neighbour; oak windows and floorboards fashioned by a carpenter six miles away.

What started as an extended holiday for Simon and Andrew has become a way of life, and it's a story that can inspire us all. For it is not just a story of giving up London's bright city lights for countryside and the stars – it's what a modern, thoughtful life can look like.

Simon Forrester & Andrew Craven

The Peren,
Lower Wyeside, Clifford,
Hay-on-Wye, HR3 5EU
● House for 5. £525-£850 p.w. Weekends (3 nights) £395-£595. Self catering.
● 01497 831225
● www.theperen.com
● Train station: Hereford

Little Quebb Cottages

HEREFORDSHIRE

Alison and John used to each give sixty hours of their week to our National Health Service. But there came a moment – when their children had grown up and they were working so hard – when they questioned what they wanted the focal point of their life to be.

Their priorities were to slow down, work for themselves, feel part of a community, find something that revolved around food. They were keen walkers and cyclists, and loved the countryside, too. The fact neither of them had any knowledge of animal husbandry, running self-catering cottages or a smallholding did not deter them from taking on the farm.

The five acres of Little Quebb Farm (the granary and barn are the self-catering parts) fitted their brief to create a peaceful retreat and an antidote to city life. "And north Herefordshire appealed because it's not on the way to anywhere," says Alison.

Guests now come to experience life on a smallholding and the greater the contrast with their everyday lives, the more heightened their enjoyment. You can help collect the eggs, feed the chunky black Berkshire pigs, pick peas and beans, gather plums, pears and apples, and heaps of soft fruits, too

"We started out hoping to be self-sufficient in vegetables within two years," says Alison. "We're not there yet – it took a while to get

used to the clay soil – but I love picking fresh beans or potatoes, and cooking them straight away."

They enrolled on day courses, read books and asked neighbouring farmers' advice on animal husbandry. "People are very generous and are far too discreet to tell us if they think we're bonkers," she says. There have been lots of tragi-comic moments: the escaped weaners that wriggled under the electric fence; the trailer bogged down in the mud on their first trip to the abattoir, the feisty pig that refused, twice, to go at all. "Tuesday is 'pig day' at the abattoir," says Alison. "A lot of batty smallholders arrive with two pigs each and as we're queuing we learn a lot from each other. It's a joy and a privilege to join in with this part of rural English life."

They never stop learning. In the lead-up to their second Christmas, family and friends formed a mini-production line for killing, plucking and eviscerating the geese. They have learnt how to make their own sausages, bacon, paté, pork pies, salamis and a Herefordshire version of Parma ham that they hang at the end of the garden. They plan to get some sheep, turkeys, quail (for the eggs) and bees and to make their own cider. The produce is not for commercial gain – it's too small-scale and too labour-intensive – "it's for ourselves, friends and guests, for fun and to share with others. We just about break even."

This home produce is found in the honesty freezer so guests can help themselves and you will find bacon ready in your own fridge. Alison and John offer dinner one night a week and breakfast on the morning of departure in the farmhouse, John is a keen cook and it's an opportunity to sample their produce. The cottages are rather bigger and more handsome than you would expect and feel generous and inviting with a light stylish touch that is neither too rustic nor off-puttingly contemporary. There are airy rooms, exposed beams, cream walls, bright plump sofas, log-burning stoves, Shaker-style kitchens, brass bedsteads and a claw-foot bath.

Solar panels provide hot water in summer, and are a good back-up in winter; the pigs eat the vegetable waste, there are compost heaps and recycling bins galore and the farm has its own

> "Our main challenges are natural ones and we don't fight them, just work with them. To see things flourish is our best reward"

borehole. As well as offering their own produce, John and Alison point guests to the local shops and markets in Kington or the farm shop at nearby Lyonshall. "It is depressing when I see the Tesco van arriving with an online shop," says Alison, who accepts she cannot dictate how guests behave.

While not dictating how people enjoy themselves, they provide an environment and an atmosphere that give people time to think. There are books, maps, guides and bicycles to borrow. "We are attuned to whether people want to chat or to be left alone," says Alison. "The pressure we were under in the NHS taught us that! But I get a huge amount of pleasure from seeing people relax."

There are walks in Eardisley and Bredwardine with its views over the river Wye – here Francis Kilvert, the Victorian country diarist, was vicar – a driving route along the 'black-and-white' villages or

the Welsh Black Mountains and Offa's Dyke for hiking. A lovely Saturday outing, says Alison, is to walk from Kington (three miles away) up to the Harp Inn gastropub at Old Radnor for lunch. Cyclists who take on Hergest Ridge get some of the best views, across Shropshire and into Wales, south to the Black Mountains and north to the little-known Radnor Forest. "For us, it's probably the best place in the world," says Alison.

Staying put often seems the best option: meandering through the garden, checking the vegetables, watching the antics of the chickens all bring deep reward. And taking a glass of wine to the end of the garden where the pigs live, sitting on the seat and watching the sun set over Hay Bluff is a fine way to end the day.

Their hours are even longer than in their previous jobs "but," says Alison, "we're at home and are our own bosses. These days our main challenges are natural ones and we don't fight them, just work with them. To see things flourish is our best reward."

Alison & John O'Grady

Little Quebb Cottages,
Little Quebb Farm,
Eardisley, HR3 6LP
- The Old Barn for 5, Granary for 4. £350–£695 p.w.
- Dinner £19.50 (by arrangement).
- 01544 327121
- www.littlequebbcottages.co.uk
- Train station: Hereford

Old Country Farm

WORCESTERSHIRE

A nightingale sings in distant woods, tawny owls duet and the night sky is liquid black, devoid of light pollution. Ella Quincy has a deep-rooted passion for the environment, and her years of commitment to Old Country Farm's eco system has made her home and her land a haven for wildlife.

In the 1930s, her father learnt about farming here. It was a primitive existence with no running water and no electricity. He loved it – as do Ella and her son Will. Her father adored trees, and bucked the trend of digging up orchards by replanting apple and pear trees in the 1940s, and keeping his hedgerows. In recent years, Ella and Will's green schemes on the two-hundred-and-twenty-acre farm continue to expand, and their educational enterprises – in the form of farm walks and courses for adults – are increasing.

Unexpected visitors have flown in. On trees, the threshing barn and even on the cider house wall, a variety of homes have been constructed: owls, tits and nuthatches have taken up residence near the house and, in the woods, a hundred bat boxes for rare Bechsteins have been nailed up and inhabited – sometimes by opportunist dormice.

From the gleaming gatehead table you spy swallows and spotted flycatchers, and a rogue squirrel stealing from the laden bird table.

Goldcrests lurk in the juniper tree, robins in the weeping pear and tree creepers in the giant redwood.

Borrow a pair of wellies, waiting by the door in many sizes, and walk out to meet the wildlife. Across the extensive lawns, your first encounter is likely to be with a family of ducks greeting you noisily from the pond.

In spring, the lawns take on a pre-Raphaelite air, delicately brushed with crocuses and cyclamens, aconites and snowdrops. Patches are then left to grow tall and wild with sorrel, cowslips and wild daffodils – and shorn for hay in the summer months.

Ducking through a natural arch, you find yourself in a secret world – a meditative garden with ferns and purple and white foxgloves. Just beyond are "Gog" and "Magog", two slumbering stone heads encircled by wild flowers. Styled on two Roman emperors, these heads were rejected from 'The Broad' – the ceremonial heart of the Oxford colleges – and bought by a don who retired to Worcestershire, then procured at auction by Ella's father and hauled back on tractor and trailer to their final resting place.

Against the dusky pink, mineral-painted walls of the house is a place of pilgrimage for horticulturalists. Ella's mother, Helen Ballard, had a reputation for breeding hellebores; here in the north border her original stock plants flourish – a hugely important collection. "Her intention

was to get flowers that stood up and looked at you, with clear colours and big, bowl-shaped flowers," says Ella. "She started in the sixties, knowing nothing about genetics, and taught herself."

Ella moved back to the fifteenth-century family home when her father died and her mother needed help, and stayed here with her two young children. The farm and family took up most of her time, but as the children flew the nest Ella decided to open up her remote and tranquil home to guests. "I thought B&B would be fun," she says.

But in many ways, Ella takes her B&B very seriously. She holds a hard-won Green Business award and relies on environmentally friendly products, from paraben-free shampoos to magnetic wash-balls. With careful research and planning, she's had built a WET (wetland ecosystem) sewage system, an impressive network of six ponds dug into the clay: these harbour millions of helpful microbes, create a pond teeming with wildlife, and prevent waste entering the water system.

Ella and her son are ardent believers in organic food and farming. Ella attended one of the first courses in organic farming in the country, grows her own vegetables and avidly supports her local suppliers. She reckons they need all the help they can get, and should 'sell' themselves more. The county has so much to offer; Ella's breakfast table is brimful of local juices, rustic breads, cheeses and Malvern organic sausages.

Two generous aunts left Ella some much-loved furniture and paintings, which make this a welcoming home. "There were lots of tables," she recalls. "All very useful now!" In one of the rustic, low-ceilinged bedrooms, her aunt's intricate patchwork quilt brightens the bed, while her battered old suitcase speaks of grand European tours.

Guests seem to unwind on arrival. One wrote: "my mother and I went to this very peaceful place in the summer. It was so relaxing – the countryside very beautiful, the bedrooms and bathrooms (one room is en suite) gorgeous, the visitors' kitchen and sitting room so well equipped, and the organic breakfasts great." You can walk to the top of the Malverns from the door, and there are a couple of bikes and helmets to borrow; Ella and Will will point to the gentle cycle routes that pass close by.

Inheriting a little of the family free spirit, Ella has embarked on the first of many potential endeavours. "It's not all solemn and heavy – that's why I've built a 'light house' in Herefordshire!" This apple-orchard retreat is a green-oak build of the highest order, vaulted to the ceiling and uplifting in every sense. A wood-burner and sheepskin rugs warm the sitting room, you eat at a long table with ash chairs, there's a snug library to retreat to for drinks and make your entertainment as you go, on the Steinway piano or guitar. Spiral up the staircase to a bedroom with a view, its balcony perched over lazily grazing sheep. Slip through glass doors to a garden and farmland that softens every edge, or stride across Ella's farm to the hills.

Her hope is that musicians, artists and anyone looking for peace and inspiration will use it. Eventually, she may choose to live there herself. Ella's own love of music is deep-rooted. Having studied it at university, her passion is listening to live music and playing herself; she prefers that to having it simply as a background. Many evenings before dinner, a trio of merry ladies gathers in the drawing room for musical evenings; Elgar's great-niece plays violin.

Ella feels she has learnt a great deal through 'coming home' and finding much-needed time and space. "Slow is about being in the moment, not worrying about external pressures. I try to listen to my intuition, to follow the path my spirit chooses for me. If I'd done everything rationally I wouldn't have achieved what I have so far."

Ella Grace Quincy

Old Country Farm,
Mathon, Malvern, WR13 5PS
- 3 rooms. £60-£90. Singles £35-£55.
  The Lighthouse for 2-10.
- 01886 880867
- www.oldcountryhouse.co.uk
- Train station: Colwall or Malvern

Annie's Cabin

SHROPSHIRE

Turn off the back road, under a huge, ageing oak tree, down into a sun-trap meadow, and you'll come across a cosy hideaway full of the subtleties of Slow living. A log cabin is an unusual building in England, especially one built by hand from great trunks of Welsh Douglas Fir, but it's such an organic structure that it fits perfectly into the meadow land by the river.

George trained originally as a forester, and his inspiration came from his stay in a cabin in the wilds of Idaho over thirty years ago. He and his partner Erica lived in a caravan in their field for three years while renovating the old mill which is now their family home. "It was like being in a hide – we could hear and see everything around us, and we missed that closeness to nature when we moved into the house," explains George. "When I came to build the cabin, I wanted to give our guests the same feeling of being part of the meadow and living with its wildlife."

He consulted with a small firm of experts based near Aberystwyth, run by friends with a forestry background in common, and started to appreciate that a log cabin responds to a Slow design approach. "Planning and building the cabin intrigued me, because wood in its unsawn, original form makes its own demands on the process. For one thing, a lot has to be decided up front, as you can't change the wall structure once it's built – no way to add on an extension, or even an extra electrical socket. In contrast, though, you can leave some things like exact positioning of windows and doors until the walls are built, so that you have a better feel for a room before cutting holes in it. Also, for me, one of the mysterious joys of the building was the fact that we could never actually draw it accurately on paper, as we didn't know beforehand how big the logs were going to be, or what distance there would be between the walls at any given point; the logs shrink too, sometimes by three or four inches over the height

of a wall, so a window, door, or anything else related to the wall has to be designed to allow the logs to move. All of these things push you gently towards taking time, doing things by eye, and keeping options open until you're sure, a Slow approach that can greatly reward any building project."

The construction and design of the cabin – named in honour of a memorable family pet – consumed George for two years. It was a labour of love, with the main aim being to maximise enjoyment for guests. The natural materials, sourced as locally as possible, create an embracing, intimate feel; as the evenings draw in, the red enamel wood-pellet stove kicks out the heat, and the sheep's wool and newspaper insulation keep the cabin snug. Chunky wooden furniture contrasts well with the deep, soft leather sofa and armchairs. The hand-made pine kitchen is Shaker in style and equipped with stylish china and green-as-can-be white goods.

"It makes sense to keep the carbon footprint of any new building minimal," says George. A Sustainable Tourism grant from Shropshire Council has helped him to install solar water heating, and he has initially chosen a green electricity tariff, but plans to add photovoltaic panels.

The sun streams in through large double-glazed gable windows and has free rein to illuminate the open-plan cabin. There's more than a touch of the modern – an impeccably equipped wet room and a state-of-the-art sound system – but, above all, this is a place that encourages simple pleasures. Take the

> "One of the mysterious joys of the building was the fact that we could never draw it accurately on paper, as we didn't know beforehand how big the logs were going to be"

guitar out through the folding door onto the boardwalk and play in the open air, or settle with a glass of wine on the south-facing terrace; at night the terraces become your stargazing spot.

The cabin is two miles (a five minute drive, or a lovely walk over fields) from Ludlow, which adds a whole extra dimension in Slow. You wander into a town which has managed to hang on to half-timbered

buildings, medieval streets and a Norman castle; and best of all, some wonderful local food which has earned the town national renown over the years. Sadly, not many English cities, let alone towns of this size, support such a choice of independent food shops; there are three butchers, four bakeries, three cheese shops, two wholefood shops, notable breweries, and regular local food markets. Two miles north of the town, in Bromfield, Ludlow Food Centre is a showcase for local produce, selling both fresh ingredients and products made on the premises. The abundance of wonderful local fresh food has also helped the area to attract top chefs, and to become famous for its exceptional restaurants.

Ludlow in 2004 became the UK's first 'Cittaslow' or 'Slow City'. The focus in all Slow towns and cities is on supporting local businesses, keeping alive regional distinctiveness, protecting the environment, welcoming visitors, calming traffic, providing convivial spaces and encouraging community activities. There are now nine Cittaslow towns in Britain and Ludlow has been charged with developing a Cittaslow network.

Back at the cabin, a well-equipped kitchen, and a shelf of cookery books may inspire you to create

your own Slow supper – wander round the food shops in the morning, get excited about your ingredients, and spend a relaxed afternoon at the cabin working up to a feast in the evening at the outdoor table by the river.

The enjoyment of his retreat brings George rich reward. "The time and money invested have been high but knowing that people are enjoying its special atmosphere is great. It reminds people that it's enjoyable to do nothing."

There's planning permission for a second cabin but George is in no hurry. "I'm thinking of something smaller, a little higher, almost a treehouse. I'd like it to be full of surprises."

George Tasker

Annie's Cabin,
Caynham Mill, Caynham, Ludlow, SY8 3BH
* Sleeps 4-6. 1 double, 1 twin, 1 double sofa bed.
* £375-£695 p.w.
* Self-catering.
* 07977 091928
* www.ludlowecologcabins.co.uk
* Train station: Ludlow

Timberstone Bed & Breakfast

SHROPSHIRE

Alex and Tracey met in the wine trade and then fell for a pair of derelict cottages. He had been a carpenter and watersports enthusiast; she had worked with a Michelin chef, Shaun Hill of the Merchant House, Ludlow. She was also a passionate traveller and had taught and worked with charities in Ghana and Belize. At Timberstone they have woven their enthusiasms together, during gaps between travels, into a whole that embraces everyone, somehow providing space for other people to be themselves.

"When we bought the house at auction, we felt as though we had signed up to living in the middle of nowhere. Ludlow wasn't famous then, and it certainly hadn't achieved gastronomic or Slow status. Now we find ourselves five miles away from Ludlow, a mecca for fresh food and passionate retailers. Best of all, there are no McDonald's or shopping malls."

Ludlow is now recognised as the Slow Food capital of the UK, it has also achieved Slow City and Fairtrade status. The town with over five hundred listed buildings hosts a famous annual food extravaganza, supports scores of artisan producers, superb butchers, enlightened retailers and a twice monthly farmers' market.

Tracey and Alex grow their own fruit and have chickens and whatever else they need they get

from local suppliers. Jams and bread are homemade, and food integrity can be measured in metres rather than food miles. The wine list is interesting, as you'd expect, the gin with your tonic is organic, and the food is delicious. Guests dine at a large communal table on twice-baked Shropshire Blue soufflés, local lamb roasted with buttery asparagus, fruit crumbles in season. It's the finest local and home-grown produce.

They are brilliant hosts, for whom nothing is too much trouble, and the interest in doing things well reaches into other corners of their lives. There is heat and hot water from a ground-source heat pump, wood-burners too, a compost heap, energy-efficient light bulbs and other ecological devices. "You have to put your money where your mouth is," says Tracey. Stacked outside are logs for the fire: hawthorn and other wood collected from the hedgerows. Alex enjoys his foraging and chopping the way other men enjoy their computers – probably more.

The inside of the house is as lovely as the outside, with touches of carefully considered luxury in curtains and quilts. There is a large family room upstairs in the top of one of the old cottages, a handsome bathroom with a huge tub and a walk-in shower lined with Welsh slate. At the other end of the house is a fine double room. And

there are numerous touches that might bring a smile to a face: charming old country pieces, books tucked into unexpected places, handles and catches devised by craftsmen. Two new rooms continue the natural feel of the place, cosy with oak floors heated underfoot. Both rooms have romantic double-ended baths and separate showers. The Clay Room has a balcony from which to catch the setting sun.

Wending your way down the wooden walkway to the bottom of the garden you come across the retreat: part Balinese, part English seaside hut, built around the four hop poles that Alex secured into the ground in an act of random but symbolic determination. The retreat has no television, just a big bed, a tiny kitchen and a bathroom. You can pour your wine, light the little barbecue and watch the sun go down. It is the family's favourite

"Stacked outside are logs for the fire: hawthorn and other wood collected from the hedgerows"

place, too, for there they can catch the morning sun on one side and the evening sun on another. When they are too busy to get away on a holiday, it becomes their retreat, their 'going away' place.

Here, too, Tracey – a trained Bowen Technique therapist and reflexologist – can minister unto her visitors. (The Bowen technique involves light moving of hands over muscles, devised to aid men in Australia returning home with war injuries.) There is also an infra-red sauna, whose health benefits include detoxification and weight loss.

Tracey's suggestions for the Slow life are simple... Choose to see the glass half full, plant something you can harvest, take a country walk, do a good deed every day, think of five things that make you smile, take a few deep breaths and exhale slowly, take the time to cook a proper meal, sit down at the table to eat as a family, switch off the TV, drink good wine, put on some music and dance!

Jack and Alfie, the two little boys, bring the place extra life. They have a play area with an evolving treehouse, and boundless enthusiasm. What is even more special is that they sweep visiting children into their circle of friendship.

Hotels and B&Bs are not always free and easy with their wellies, bikes and binoculars. Tracey and Alex are and, though you may relax in the garden with a good book, there is more to do in this area than an army of visitors could absorb: castles, gardens, hill walks, the races and Ironbridge Gorge. In the shadow of Clee Hill, you can take off straight from the door in almost any direction on foot, up hedge-rowed lanes fringed with cow parsley.

"This is the life style we have chosen. We welcome people into our home because we love it." That is Tracey talking, but they both feel it.

Tracey Baylis & Alex Read

Timberstone Bed & Breakfast,
Clee Stanton, Ludlow, SY8 3EL
- 4 rooms.
- £87.50–£125. Singles from £45.
- Dinner, 3 courses, £24.50. Licensed.
- 01584 823519
- www.timberstoneludlow.co.uk
- Train station: Ludlow.

Manor Farm

DERBYSHIRE

"After deciding we wouldn't lamb this year, Simon got broody," laughs Gilly, "so he went out one day and came back with a handful of in-lamb Jacob ewes."

The Grooms strike a fine balance running their farmhouse, production company, and all the activities at this beautiful working farm that sits within the World Heritage area of Derbyshire. They both acknowledge that "we have the best of all worlds".

The historic hamlet of Dethick has a medieval ambience. Aside from a tiny church and the two other farmhouses, the only neighbours are sheep, cows and a secret world of happy wildlife.

The Grade II* listed farmhouse rests above a patchwork of flower-filled hay meadows, natural woodland and lush green fields nibbled by lazy sheep and bordered by miles of ancient dry-stone walls. Skylarks, curlews, swallows and hawks crisscross wide skies above.

Simon's family has owned the 165-acre farm for sixty years. Their legacy shows in the stone-walled landscape of fields and meadows embroidered with ancient hedgerows and wildflowers and alive with animals and birds.

Simon and Gilly are intent upon preserving all this and adding to it, keeping sheep typical to Derbyshire – mules mostly - and a new herd of Hereford cattle. Newly planted areas of native woodland: horse

chestnut, holly, ash, wild cherry, oak, beech and hazel sit in ancient woodland and you can ramble among them all on a family-friendly walk the couple has mapped out.

Small groups are welcome for tailor-made activities. One tutor teaches Bushcraft Skills: making natural shelters, spinning string from nettles and honing wood into mallets. But it's not just nature that draws people here. Dethick is drenched in history, a magical tapestry of secrets and stories that imbue the surroundings with an atmosphere rich in memory and meaning. The house overlooks the pretty church of St John the Baptist, built by the Dethicks in 1228.

The estates passed from Dethicks to Babingtons but in 1586 Anthony Babington was hanged, drawn and quartered after a failed plot to rescue the imprisoned Mary Queen of Scots and instate her on the throne of England, after assassinating Queen Elizabeth I. "We are still discovering fascinating new things, including the remains of the original Tudor garden, right in front of the house."

The magnificent Tudor kitchen dates back to 1403, with its twelve-foot-high ceilings, beams and stone archways astride an enormous fireplace around which the house was rebuilt in 1670. It's an experience to breakfast where, for six hundred years, generations have lived and worked.

Gilly uses local and organic ingredients for her breakfasts, fruits from their garden turned into wonderful compôtes and honey from Simon's fathers hives. Her ever-changing menus offers a traditional farmhouse breakfast and fish and vegetarian dishes or specials such as Derbyshire Oatcakes and hot smoked salmon. You can have a breakfast picnic in the garden or churchyard next door, or even have it delivered to your room anytime until eleven.

In order to give guests more room to simply 'be' – Simon and Gilly have just put the final polish on the east wing. They've added three bedrooms two up in the old hayloft, a disabled access room downstairs and a meeting space in the former calf house.

The restoration of this listed building was a mighty task but the couple were adamant that traditional materials must adhere to their eco-sustainable principles. Lime plastered walls are lined with recycled wood and the roof space insulated with sheep's wool. Beams and purlins were restored and heavy oak window headers were sourced from their own oak, hewn and seasoned by Simon's father years before. Heating and hot water will be powered by an air source heat pump.

Simon and Gilly had long careers in the BBC and their journalistic backgrounds and innate curiosities mean they each hold a wealth of knowledge about Derbyshire. Although Simon grew up at Dethick, he also enthuses about the regeneration of the city of Derby, its restored shopping lanes and riverside development and its new visual arts centre QUAD. (Simon is an official Ambassador for Derby and an unofficial one for Derby County football team). If you arrive by train, one of them will collect you from Cromford's pretty restored station; Gilly can point you in the direction of stately homes and tea shops or give you one of her own visitor trails or maps with walking routes. She'll arrange cycle hire or explain how to get to Chatsworth House by bus. In the evening, stroll across their fields to the Jug and Glass Inn - Florence Nightingale's first hospital.

Alison Uttley (creator of Little Grey Rabbit and Sam Pig) recorded her childhood reminiscenses and early life at Castle Top Farm just over the hill. Her

children's story 'A Traveller in Time' was based on Manor Farm which she renamed 'Thackers'.

"I see the beautiful countryside with its woods and gentle hills stretching out infinitely green, and the little brook shimmering with sunlight as it flows under the hazel groves. I hear the murmer of woodpigeons, sleepy and monotonous in the beech wood, and the warm intimate call of the cuckoo in the orchard by the house. Ice-cold water springs from the mossy earth... I smell the hot scents of the herb garden drenched in sunshine, and the perfume of honeysuckle after rain, but stronger than these is the rich fragrance of the old house, made up of wood-smoke, haystacks and old old age, mingled together indissolubly".

Look for Uttley's 'Old Farmhouse Recipes', filled with curious recipes such as Canary Pudding and Beestings Cakes. "The recipes are based around seasonal foods. There were no supermarkets or factory farms in Uttley's day." Mercifully there is no evidence of them here today.

Gilly & Simon Groom

Manor Farm,
Dethick, Matlock, DE4 5GG
- 5: 2 doubles, 1 twin/double/family; 1 twin/double on the ground floor.
- £70-£85. Singles £45-£55.
- 01629 534302
- www.manorfarmdethick.co.uk
- Train station: Cromford

Yorkshire   Cumbria   Northumberland

ENGLAND: NORTH

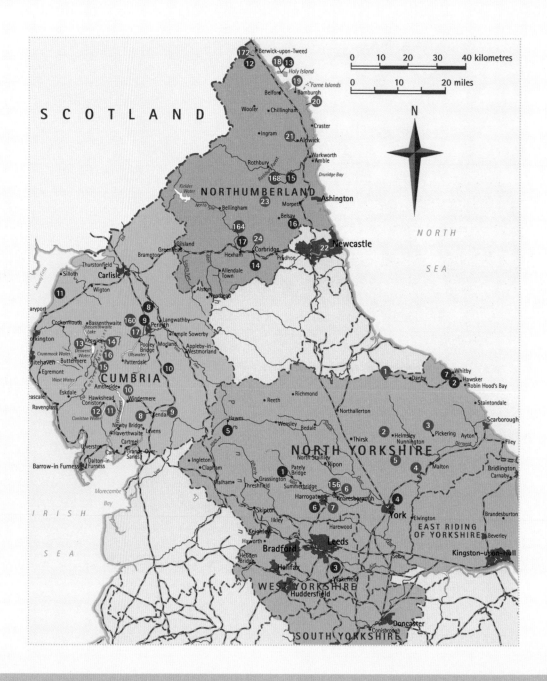

SCOTLAND

Berwick-upon-Tweed

172
18 13
12
Holy Island
19 Farne Islands
20 Bamburgh
Belford
Wooler Chillingham
Craster
Ingram
21 Alnwick
Rothbury Warkworth
Amble
Druridge Bay
Kielder Water
168 15
NORTHUMBERLAND
23 Ashington
Bellingham Morpeth
Belsay
164 16
Gilsland Greenhead
17 24 Corbridge
Brampton Hexham
Prudhoe 22 **Newcastle**
14
Allendale Town
Alston
Nenthead
Thurstonfield
Carlisle
Wigton
11
Maryport

0 10 20 30 40 kilometres
0   10   20 miles

N

NORTH

SEA

Cockermouth Bassenthwaite
160 9 Penrith Langwathby
Bassenthwaite Lake
rkington 13 14 17 Temple Sowerby
Derwent Water Keswick Pooley Appleby-in-
16 Bridge Morland Westmorland
Crummock Water Ullswater
hitehaven Buttermere 15 Patterdale
Egremont West Water **CUMBRIA** 10
ascale Ambleside
Ravenglass 10 Windermere
Hawkshead Coniston
Eskdale
12 11 Kendal 9
Coniston Water Newby Bridge 8
Haverthwaite Levens
Uverston Cartmel Grange-over-
Cark Sands
Grange-over-
Barrow-in-Furness Dalton-in-
Furness
Morecambe Bay

IRISH

SEA

1 Whitby
Danby 7 Hawsker
2 Robin Hood's Bay
Staintondale
Reeth Richmond
Northallerton
Scarborough
Bawes Wensley Bedale 3
5 2 Helmsley Pickering Ayton
Thirsk Nunnington Filey
NORTH YORKSHIRE
North Stainley 5
Ripon 4 Malton
Ingleton 1 Pately Bridgington
Clapham Bridge Carnaby
Malham Grassington 4
Threshfield Summerbridge Brandesburton
156 6 York Beverley
Harrogate Knaresborough 4 Elvington
Skipton 6 7 **EAST RIDING**
Ilkley **OF YORKSHIRE**
Harewood Kingston-upon-Hull
Keighley
Haworth **Leeds**
Hebden **Bradford** Selby
Bridge
Halifax 3
WEST YORKSHIRE Wakefield
Huddersfield

Doncaster
Conisbrough
SOUTH YORKSHIRE

1 Slow travel   1 Slow food   1 Special places to stay (with page numbers)

ENGLAND: NORTH

Slow travel

1. Roseberry Topping
2. Walk from Rievaulx Abbey to Byland Abbey
3. North Yorkshire Moors Railway
4. Castle Howard
5. Masham Sheep Fair
6. Knaresborough
7. Harrogate
8. Abbot Hall Art Gallery
9. Farfield Mill
10. Jesus Church
11. Brantwood
12. Swallows & Amazons Cruise
13. Nichol End Marine
14. Keswick Railway Walk
15. Galleny Force
16. Theatre by the Lake
17. Greystoke Cycle Café
18. Holy Island
19. Bamburgh Beach & Castle
20. The Farne Islands
21. The Alnwick Garden
22. The Biscuit Factory
23. Elsdon
24. Corbridge

Slow food

1. The Oldest Sweet Shop in England
2. Colmans Fish & Chips
3. E Oldroyd & Sons
4. York Food Festival
5. Wensleydale Creamery
6. Betty's Café Tearooms
7. Mister Chips
8. The Village Bakery
9. Dalemain Marmalade Festival
10. Orton Farmers' Market
11. Cumbrian Food Safari
12. Chain Bridge Honey Farm
13. St Aidan's Winery
14. Brocksbushes Farm
15. Corner Shop
16. The Northumberland Cheese Company Ltd
17. Hexham Farmers' Market

Special places to stay (with page numbers)

Slow travel

1 Roseberry Topping
Newton-under-Roseberry
(01642 328901)
320-metre high and worth every puff for the 360-degree view from the summit: to Whitby and the sea one way, the Yorkshire Dales t'other.

2 Walk from Rievaulx Abbey to Byland Abbey
Not one but two ruined abbeys on the North York Moors, with an atmospheric six-mile walk between them. Reward yourself by stopping off at the Abbey Inn (01347 868204) fifty paces from Byland's door.
www.english-heritage.org.uk

3 North Yorkshire Moors Railway
(01751 472508)
From Pickering to Whitby and back again, steam-chuffing your way through the ruggedly beautiful North York Moors. August is heather heaven.
www.nymr.co.uk

4 Castle Howard
Near Malton (01653 648444)
There's a divertingly lovely farm shop with all manner of regional food and drink – and the Palladian Castle and gardens are captivating, too.
www.castlehoward.co.uk

5 Masham Sheep Fair
In September in this pretty market town, featuring a cast of thousands. Gambling types might fancy a flutter on the 200 yard sweepstake when woolly racers sprint to the post lured by buckets of feed.
www.visitmasham.com

6 Knaresborough
Hire boats in yet another pretty market town and wend your way up the river Nidd, marvelling at the castle and the spectacular viaduct on the way. Buy some toffees at Farrah's on Market Place, housed in what was the oldest chemist's shop in England, established in 1720.
www.knaresborough.co.uk

7 Harrogate
Lavender-laundered Harrogate is famous for Betty's Tea Rooms – but you could also take a soak in the lovely, old-worldly and communal Turkish baths, buy some period furnishings in Montpellier, and listen to the band play in Valley Gardens in summer.

8 Abbot Hall Art Gallery
Kendal (01539 722464)
Entrancing Georgian house with café on the banks of the river Kent with an impressive programme of temporary exhibitions alongside a permanent collection.
www.abbothall.org.uk

9 Farfield Mill
Sedbergh (015396 21958)
Converted textile mill with 15 artist studios, contemporary crafts, power looms worked by master weaver at weekends, and lunches and brunches in the Weavers Café. Felt and textiles workshops too.

10 Jesus Church
Troutbeck
A place for quiet contemplation. The east window, designed by Edward Burne-Jones with additions by Ford Maddox Brown and William Morris, is inspiring.

11 Brantwood
Coniston (015394 41396)
Lakeside home of the Victorian writer, artist, thinker and early conservationist John Ruskin, now a lively centre of arts. Acres of gardens with spectacular views cling to the rocky slopes - fabulous.
www.brantwood.org.uk

12 Swallows & Amazons Cruise
Coniston Water (015394 36216)
All aboard the 1920's solar-electric launch for a watery exploration of the places that inspired Arthur Ransome to write his classic children's book - remember Holly Howe, Kanchenjunga and Wild Cat Island?
www.conistonlaunch.co.uk

13 Nichol End Marine
Portinscale (017687 73082)
Catch a boat around Derwent Water, hire a dinghy, windsurfer or kayak, fish for pike, bream and

trout – all is possible from this pretty bay. Breakfasts, soups and scones at the café, revived after the floods of 2009.
www.nicholendmarine.co.uk

14 Keswick Railway Walk
A two-hour circular walk for non-fitties, from little Threlkeld across lush pastures to Westcoewith, then down to the trackbed of the old railway, via viaducts and tunnel, and back to the pub at Threlkeld.
www.walkingworld.com

15 Galleny Force
Wild swimming in the tumbling Galleny at the head of Borrowdale. Two fairy glen pools, with silver birches and ferns, frame a stunning Lakeland scene.

16 Theatre by the Lake
Keswick (017687 74411)
A great programme of events year round but the summer season is the highlight – and you're on the edge of Derwent Water. Keswick bustles with trekkers and outdoor adventurers all year.
www.theatrebythelake.com

17 Greystoke Cycle Café
Greystoke (01768 483984)
A lovely garden for lunch or tea – much organic. Summer sees a 'cyclists barn' replete with towels, blankets, drinks and flapjacks (honesty box). Brilliant for cold wet bikers, and workshops, too – willow weaving, drystone walling.
www.greystokecyclecafe.co.uk

18 Holy Island
Atmospheric tidal island reached via a causeway (watch for closing times!), credited with being the birthplace of Christianity. Lindisfarne Castle was transformed by Lutyens into an Edwardian holiday home, with a walled garden designed by Gertrude Jekyll. Plus: renovated upturned boats that allow you to experience the interior of a 19th-century herring drifter.
www.lindisfarne.org.uk

19 Bamburgh Beach & Castle
A vast, big-skies beach overlooked by an equally impressive castle (01668 214515) perched on an outcrop. The Grace Darling Museum (01668 214910) is in Bamburgh, too.
www.bamburghcastle.com

20 The Farne Islands
Billy Shiel's family have been taking visitors from Seahouses to the Farme Islands since 1918. You'll spot an astonishing array of wildlife as you cruise, with grey seals and puffins galore.
www.farne-islands.com

21 The Alnwick Garden
Alnwick (01665 511350)
Forget about decking and quick fixes as you wander the Duchess of Northumberland's visionary creation. Gardening on a grand scale.
www.alnwickgarden.com

22 The Biscuit Factory
Newcastle Upon Tyne
(0191 261 1103)
Britain's biggest original art store with two floors of exhibition space and two of artists' studios. You can arrange art hire, too. Lunch smartly at the buzzing Brasserie Black Door (0191 260 5411).

23 Elsdon
Walk down a long, lonely road between Elsdon and Cambo high in the Redesdale hills, shiver at the hangman's gibbet on the way. Elsdon's small 14th-century church is said to be haunted. If you're here at the end of August try the village fete for some more down-to-earth fun.

24 Corbridge
Corbridge has long been regarded as a great place for idling away the day shopping. Don't miss Re-found Objects (01434 634567; closed Mondays): it's stylishly laid out and sells recycled, reclaimed and rescued objects of usefulness and beauty.
www.re-foundobjects.com

Slow food

1 The Oldest Sweet Shop in England
Pateley Bridge (01423 712371)
In the unmissable Dales, an unmissable purveyor of humbugs and liquorice, silver almonds and sherbet lemons, tigernuts and toffee brazils. Closed Mon/Tues.

2 Colmans Fish & Chips (est. 1905)
South Shields (0191 4561202)
Gourmet fish 'n' chips near the beach. Cod, turbot, whiting from sustainable fishing grounds and Maris Piper chips, fried in additive-free oil that's turned (later) into bio fuel. Great fish cakes, crab cakes, battered squid too.

3 E Oldroyd & Sons
Rothwell (0113 2822245)
Forced rhubarb is grown in dark sheds and picked by candlelight – find out more on a tour with Janet Oldroyd Hulme, High Priestess of Rhubarb.
www.yorkshirerhubarb.co.uk

4 York Food Festival
York (01904 466687)
Late September markets, cookery workshops, tutored tastings and all manner of events.
www.yorkfoodfestival.com

5 Wensleydale Creamery
Hawes (01969 667664)
Say cheese or even taste cheese – restaurant, shop and viewing gallery. Wallace and Gromit's favourite cheese has been made in Wensleydale since 1150.
www.wensleydale.co.uk

6 Betty's Café Tearooms
Harrogate (01423 877300)
An institution and rightly so. Elegance, afternoon tea and the infamous Warm Yorkshire Fat Rascals.
www.bettys.co.uk

7 Mister Chips
Whitby (01947 604683)
One can only wonder at Captain Cook's wanderlust when he was apprenticed in wonderful Whitby. Tuck into proper fish and chips.
www.misterchipswhitby.co.uk

8 The Village Bakery
Melmerby (01768 898437)
Breads baked at this pioneering bakery are based on the motto "time equals flavour", a slow maxim if ever there was one. A restaurant with a gallery above and a shop.
www.village-bakery.com

9 Dalemain Marmalade Festival
Dalemain (017684 86450)
February fun and marmalade, to the backdrop of a magnificent mansion. Over 800 jars from marmalade hopefuls are tested and tried.
www.marmaladefestival.com

10 Orton Farmers' Market
In pretty Orton, on the second Saturday of the month, 9.30am–2pm. Nearby Pooley Bridge Market is held on the last Sunday of the month, April–September.
www.ortonfarmers.co.uk

11 Cumbrian Food Safari
(01900 881356)
Get chauffeur-driven around the Lake District by local-food champion Annette Gibbons.
www.cumbriaonaplate.co.uk

12 Chain Bridge Honey Farm
Horncliffe (01289 386362)
Bees from 2,000 hives, within a 40-mile radius from Berwick, forage on rape, hawthorn, willowherb borage, phacelia and heather. Watch a living colony behind glass, tuck into honey ice cream in the double decker bus café, walk to the historic Union Chain Bridge.

13 St Aidan's Winery
Holy Island (01289 389230)
Mead is reputed to be one of the world's oldest alcoholic drinks and an aphrodisiac. Still made on the island. Winery showroom open throughout the season.
www.lindisfarne-mead.co.uk

14 Brocksbushes Farm
Corbridge (01434 633100)
May your basket overflow with strawberries, raspberries, tayberries and more at this gorgeously situated pick-your-own farm. Cream teas too.
www.brocksbushes.co.uk

15 Corner Shop
Longframlington (01665 570241)
A proper village shop with a true gentleman at the helm. David Carr stocks everything his community could wish for, and rises four days a week before dawn to source the freshest and best.

16 The Northumberland Cheese Company Ltd
Blagdon (01670 789798)
Award-winning producers with shop and café serving curd tarts, cheese scones and more.
www.northumberlandcheese.co.uk

17 Hexham Farmers' Market
Hexham (07963 426932)
Second and fourth Saturday of the month, 9am–1.30pm, in the Market Place with the abbey as backdrop. Universally acclaimed.
www.hexhamfarmersmarket.co.uk

Pubs & inns

Shoulder of Mutton

Kirkby Overblow, Yorkshire
Handsome old inn, hub of the village, with far-reaching views from its child-friendly garden. Find guest ales and dedication in the kitchen: tuck into updated pub classics. Pub shop sells scrumptious pies. 01423 871205

King's Arms

Heath, Yorkshire
In a dark rich network of tap rooms, hissing gas lamps cast an amber glow on panelled walls, blackened range and coal fires. Attached is a serviceable restaurant for trad pub grub; gardens have moorland views. 01924 377527

Old Crown

Heston Newmarket, Cumbria
A dreamy village, and porter on tap! Owned by a cooperative of 147 souls, the famously authentic pub offers darts, settles, books, coal fires and great beers brewed at the back. Curries and Sunday roasts too. 01697 478288

White Hart

Bouth, Cumbria
Taxidermy and tankards in this sleepy village local. Delicious no-nonsense menu offers small portions for children, black leather sofas front long-fuelled stoves, and shooting parties gather on winter Saturdays. 01229 861229

Queens Head Hotel

Troutbeck, Cumbria
Majestic views on the Kirkstone pass - and woodsmoke and a warren of fascinating rooms. Ramblers tuck into hearty suppers of slow-braised lamb and sticky toffee pudding as dogs doze. Fine beers, too. 01539 432174

Tower Bank Arms

Sawrey, Cumbria
Next to Beatrix Potter's farm is Jemima Puddleduck's inn. Flowers and shining bits and bobs make the place homely, Cumbrian dishes please walkers and courteous National Trust staff handle the summer crowds. 01539 436334

Ship Inn

Low Newton by Sea, Northumberland
Authentic coastal inn with old settles, a solid-fuel stove and home brewed beer. Crab rolls and lobster from over the way, free-range ham and fairtrade coffee. Park back from the beach; step back a hundred years. 01665 576282

Barrasford Arms

Barrasford, Northumberland
A substantial inn with a sheltered garden close to Hadrian's Wall. They purchase a rare-breed pig each week, for sausages and sublime crackling; beer is from High House Farm. Frequented by farmers and fishermen. Ace. 01434 681232

Queens Head Inn

Great Whittington, Northumberland
A warm refuge in a wild country of moors, sheep and vast skies. Toast your toes from the carved oak settle before the fire, then tuck into wonderful food from the best available produce. Both pub and staff are charming. 01434 672267

Gallon House

YORKSHIRE

This is the Vale of York, lush and fertile, an ancient passageway for Romans, Cavaliers and pursuing Roundheads, with a limestone ridge that has offered up the handsome stone for many a fine building, including York Minster. The river Nidd, in the gorge far below, curls round a sandstone cliff; from Gallon House you are poised above it all.

Sue, a Knaresborough girl, was working at the famous tea shop, Betty's, in Harrogate, and needed a chef to train the staff. "Along came the gorgeous, immaculate Rick – pristine and in his whites. He was charming and an instant hit with everyone. Soon after that we started going out together. That was 15 years ago. They married just after moving in here, went on honeymoon and when they returned wondered what on earth they had done. The place was awash with pink and avocado bathroom suites. So their achievements are remarkable, and should help qualify Knaresborough as a new gastro mecca.

They have turned a grim old guest house, built in 1835, into an eccentric-looking yet contemporary B&B that somehow manages to pulse with both energy and calm. They named it Gallon House after John Gallon who owned the flax mill below, reached by Gallon Steps from the back of the house, a challenging climb. The mill is a reminder that Knaresborough was prosperous, as are the Georgian houses that dominate the narrow streets and alleys. The town is not unlike Durham, with its impressive railway viaduct that once, impossibly, brought the vulgar steam engine and its tourist hordes to a sleepy town. The station is just a minute from Gallon House, so you need no car. The pace of life in the house will take you over, followed by the food, Rick's special passion. He used to own and run restaurants, but now much prefers this less hectic pace.

Rick's father was a farmer but Rick went to catering college rather than back to the farm, preparing animals for the table, not raising them. He learned his craft at

Extra pictures: Colin Poole

the Imperial Hotel in Torquay, the Box Tree in Ilkley, and later in Florida. His family owned brasseries and hotels in Harrogate before he left to come here.

The Gallon's menu is varied and enticing. Gracing the big oak table at breakfast time are fruit compotes in cinnamon syrup, homemade muesli, grilled Whitby kippers, bacon muffins, and, if you are undaunted by serious excess, you can have a traditional Yorkshire breakfast instead, with Rick's homemade black pudding. "Cooking is generally quite simple, it only looks complicated, but it has to have love in it." For dinner, after a glass of sherry, there may be caramelised onion and tomato tart, herb-encrusted chicken breasts, a light summer pudding; such things are the tip of an impressive culinary iceberg. Rick has spent forty years as a chef, and is remarkably fit; a hard-working chef can easily

"Cooking is generally quite simple, it only looks complicated, but has to have love in it"

walk seven miles in a day, careering about in the kitchen. He is also a keen cyclist, one of the John O' Groats to Land's End brethren and a committed supporter of Sustrans, the cycling charity that has done so much to restore our confidence in cycling as a viable means of transport – as well as a Slow path to happiness.

Time spent trawling local markets and suppliers and admiring glistening wild trout, wiggly asparagus, rhubarb as pink as Blackpool rock is well spent. "I grew interested in Slow Food about eight years ago, hearing about it on the radio. I totally subscribe to its principles, and it is now very much a low carbon footprint movement too." Finding good ingredients is a big part of what Rick does. It's a far cry from the 80s, when restaurants vied with each other to introduce the most exotic ingredients out of season. Sue points out another aspect of Slow living: the willingness to work with other people. She would

love to run courses on this very subject – and probably will. She is a determined woman, with Yorkshire grit as well as charm.

They have done colourful and comfortable things to the house's interior. In your snug room with a view of castle or river you'll find a bottle of Black Sheep Ale from Masham, Yorkshire Tea and Taylor's roast coffee, along with Harrogate Spa water (historic Harrogate is ten minutes by train). The conservatory is bright and sunny, with views over the gorge and river, a tiled floor to echo the creams and terracottas of the hall, big pots and plants and a table for tea. There's a Cornish harbour scene by John Maltby (with moving boat parts), and if you have lost touch with the National Geographic magazine you can drift back through thirty years worth of them. The sitting room has a huge fireplace decked out with candles, original oak panelling and irresistible sofas.

If you are here in August you will witness the Knaresborough Feva, a colourful festival of entertainment and visual arts. Sue and Rick organise themed evenings: up to twenty-four locals feasting in the conservatory and dining room. They enjoy being involved in the community, so much so that Rick has volunteered to be a fireman.

Knaresborough has one last claim to fame: Mother Shipton, England's most famous prophetess who lived at the time of Henry VIII and foretold the attempted invasion by, and subsequent defeat of, the Spanish Armada in 1588. She also gave forewarning, Samuel Pepys tells us, of the Great Fire of London, but must have been ignored.

Sue & Rick Hodgson

Gallon House,
47 Kirkgate, Knaresborough, HG5 8BZ
* 3 rooms.
* £120. Singles £85.
* Dinner, 3 courses, £32.
* 01423 862102
* www.gallon-house.co.uk
* Train station: Knaresborough

Daffodil & Daisy

CUMBRIA

The great poet William Wordsworth lived for several years on the southern edge of these rugged, lyrical landscapes. How could they fail to fire his prose and nurture his creativity? Nothing can diminish the primeval sensuality of these plush green mountains, their necklaces of streams running down to the jewel-like lakes, the echoing hills and sheep-dotted valleys, the dreamy villages.

When her third child was born, Teen (short for Catriona) suddenly found the city air was suffocating her; she needed more sky and wanted to grow her own food, sustainably. She is a local girl, born and bred in Cumbria, on the northern boundary of the Lake District National Park, who flew away to join British Airways for fourteen years before coming back to Cumbria and founding a family.

So they looked for a place that was part of the soaring countryside, not too far from family and with a real sense of community. Set among echoing hills and unblemished countryside, Banks Farm had been a sheep farm for over four centuries. It was built in 1678 and has the iconic hills and fell tops of Blencathra on its doorstep, wandering wild lakeland ponies and views across the sea to Scotland.

They received a two-hundred-and-thirty-year-old moving-in gift from their predecessors: wedged between two stones they found a letter written in the 1780s by an illegitimate son to his father, the Banks Farm incumbent, announcing that, with no hope of any inheritance, he was setting off to make his fortune in the West Indies.

Teen and David converted to small-holding with delight. "Here, your soul can sing," says Teen, "and it's so good to share the peace and beauty. We did just the right thing in opening Daffodil and Daisy to guests. It's rewarding to welcome people here and

I love spending time getting the cottages ready, filling the rooms with garden flowers from the garden."

People who come appreciate the space outside to enjoy the beauty of their surroundings and the privacy they have in their generous suites, too. The feel is a mix of rustic and boutique: rooms are in calm whites, taupes and creams, Italian marbled floors gleam and bathrooms come with a generous supply of indulging lotions and potions.

The food is a draw, too. David and Teen lovingly nurture the slow-growing free-roaming Hebridean sheep who become meat at eighteen months instead of the usual six. "It's incomparable," is Teen's opinion, "and Raymond Blanc says Hebridean is the best lamb there is." "Our traditional English Saddleback pigs make pork that tastes different, too. We make everything ourselves, except bacon. We've found a fabulous twenty-four-hour recipe for roasting pork." After buying tiny gosling chicks for

> "We are learning together and hope we are helping our children to discover a sustainable existence that they will want to pursue in later life"

fattening, they are now rearing their own geese. "We kept two back last Christmas who turned out to be male and female; the goose lays eggs that make two-person omelettes.

"The wonderful thing is that our children, now seven, five and three, take it all for granted. They help us dig the garden, plant flowers, sow vegetables. We're all learning together. They understand where – or who – their food comes from. We really hope we are helping them to discover a sustainable existence that they will want to pursue into later life."

The fruit trees they planted three years ago are thriving and they delight in sharing their home-grown triumphs with guests. Guests are greeted with homemade scones and delicious breakfasts of fruit,

local kippers, salmon and scrambled eggs or the full works with their own Cumberland Sausages and bacon and black and white puddings from Charles Macleod of Stornoway on the Isle of Lewis.

Despite the sense of peace and space, Bank Farm is very much part of a community "that," says Teen, "has a real heart and truly works. Our cottage pub, The Old Crown, is collectively owned by the community, the first of its kind as far as we know. It's a focal point for us all and nourishes the community spirit: we take pleasure in introducing our guests to it." Teen is a robust supporter of their little local school that has just sixty-five pupils; David and Teen have, it is clear, taken the Cumbrian landscape and the community to their hearts.

This is fabulous walking and bicycling country, the coast-to-coast path almost passes the door. Come by train, bike or on foot and you will earn a ten per cent discount and Teen will collect you from Penrith station.

Teen & David Fisher

Daffodil & Daisy, Banks Farm,
Hesket Newmarket,
Near Penrith, CA7 8HR
- 2 rooms. £150. Single £110.
- Meals, from £15.
- 01697 478137
- www.daffodilbanksfarm.co.uk
- Train station: Penrith

Southlands Farm

NORTHUMBERLAND

The scenery is awe-inspiring and the skies huge. Here the World Heritage site of Hadrian's Wall, the Roman Emperor's frontier that links South Shields on the east coast and Ravenglass on the west, is particularly impressive. Much of the original seventy-three-mile-long wall that took three legions of Roman soldiers six years to build remains. The vastness and the emptiness of the landscape conspire to make you slow down, feel insignificant and closer to nature.

Charles wants to offer people "a reconnection between land and food, human health and wellbeing – the connection that supermarkets, takeaways, motorways and air miles have almost obliterated".

Dee and Charles remember how one of their very first guests, a little boy, convinced them of the worth of their new venture: he thought it magical to meet the hen who would lay his breakfast egg.

"Some people just want a holiday but others want to become involved and help," he says. "There's nothing so much fun as showing people things that they haven't tried before." There was the psychiatrist, whose job was treating drug addicts, who wanted to learn to shoot a rabbit. He did so, skinned it and cooked it for supper. Then there was the accountant who, after Dee introduced him to Northumberland's antique markets, switched careers to become an antiques dealer.

For Dee and Charles, who have owned the thirty-seven-acre smallholding at Gunnerton for twenty-one years, it's been a gradual life change. Both are from Northumbrian country-loving stock but Dee began their married life as a fashion student in 1988 designing wedding dresses while Charles, after doing an agricultural course and spell of shepherding in New Zealand, had taken to restoring classic cars. Charles became uneasy about the "waste" of cars and began converting them to LPG. "I became more concerned and more determined to live differently. I decided I could do much more if we got the farm back in hand."

So, the fields (pesticide- and fertiliser-free) were stocked with Kune Kune pigs and Dexter cows while the courtyard flapped with hens; back went the hawthorn hedgerows, in went native trees and in 2010 a batch of orphaned lambs arrived. Raised vegetable beds were added and a splendid 1950s greenhouse installed.

Charles's workshops, the eighteenth-century sandstone byre and granary, were converted into three self-catering cottages with Charles doing much of the planning and fitting out. The wrought-iron curtain and hanging rails (he's also an artisan blacksmith), are his handiwork, too.

Dee's keen eye for colour and design has created spaces that are

light, breezy and full of country freshness without being twee: creamy walls and throws on sofas, embroidered quilts and bright-patterned rugs; chunky farmhouse tables and pine linen presses. Exposed beams, handmade kitchens, wood-burning stoves and open fires bump up the rustic comfort.

Guests drift across to the courtyard garden with its ancient feeding troughs overflowing with lavender and roses, as if pulled by an invisible thread, to look at the vegetable garden. There, lettuces and courgettes, broccoli and onions and heritage potatoes grow. "We're pretty much self-sufficient in vegetables and people can help themselves," says Dee. "One German family dug up some carrots, cancelled the day's plans and raced back into the cottage to make soup!" In October there are sloes to pick and take home knowing that, with the simple addition of gin and sugar, they'll make an exceptional gin for Christmas.

At various times piglets, lambs and calves arrive and, inevitably, there are sausages, bacon, ham, lamb and beef to buy. There is an 'honesty freezer', along with shelves of other local produce.

Dee encourages people to use the village shop at Barrasford and the farmers' market at Hexham. "It would be easier to go to a supermarket, but it is great if people consider other options," she says.

People take gifts and ideas home with them: maybe cuttings from the garden, ideas about installing their own solar panels and vows never again to eat supermarket meat; one family returned with the news that they now kept hens, too.

You may find the time to read or snooze in the garden: there is something about the atmosphere here that permits idle pursuits. Compare bird-spotting notes with Charles – he's a naturalist – or ask about learning to fly-fish; the McGowan family, including son, Hector, and daughter, Rosie, are experts and will take you to the nearby North Tyne. You could, too, learn more about painting from Dee or try your hand on Charles's blacksmithing anvil.

Gunnerton Nick Nature Reserve is a walk away and is splendid with orchids in early summer. There is a walk, too, along the old railway line from

the farm to Wark on the North Tyne and a magical walk up to Money Hill the site of a twelfth-century Norman motte and bailey castle. A dedicated bus runs along Hadrian's wall so you can dip in and out.

Charles' and Dee's lives are full of the unexpected – life with animals is like that. There are early feeds, nights broken by difficult births, escaped Dexters to capture. "If I let anything slip, it's the admin," says Charles. "Even on bad days, I find something uplifting.

"What we do is a way of living rather than a job," he says. "Each activity contributes to a much bigger picture. The re-laid hedgerows, for example, have attracted more birds; low-level grazing has encouraged wild meadow flowers; we've created work for a gardener and extra business for the village shop." And they have plans to install a wind turbine.

"By letting people share our lifestyle we can push our dreams," says Dee. "Our life has even more purpose if other people can share it."

Dee & Charles McGowan

Southlands Farm: East, West & Middle Cottages, Gunnerton, Hexham, NE48 4EA
- East Cottage, sleeps 4; Middle Cottage, sleeps 2; West Cottage, sleeps 4.
- £300-£800 per week. Short breaks available.
- 01434 681464/07900 271455
- www.southlandsfarmcottages.co.uk
- Train station: Hexham

Thistleyhaugh

NORTHUMBERLAND

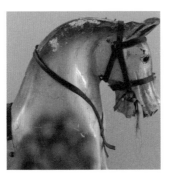

We are told that at best farmers are unappreciated, at worst, held in low esteem. What a delight, then, deep in the heart of Northumberland, to encounter a farmer who loves his job, who is successful at it, and whose family flourishes around him. The farm has been in Henry's family for over a hundred years, and in its current shape since 1780.

So fearful of Scottish raiders were the Northumbrians that the eighteenth century produced few buildings up here that were built for pure pleasure. Older history of this land reveals Saxon settlers, and then the Danes who pillaged, ravaged, plundered and then settled so much of old Northumbria. They resisted the feudalism that emerged elsewhere, preferring a free peasantry – though great estates flourished later. They brought, too, their customs, such as their duodecimal system of counting in twelves, rather than tens. Much of the special character of the northeast is owed to the Danish mix, and anthropologists have found powerful DNA connections between Geordies and modern Vikings, so the mix is verified.

There are 300 Welsh Black and Aberdeen Angus beef cattle and 1,500 ewes gently chewing their way through the 720 acres that are Thistleyhaugh. Guinea fowl, ducks, hens and pigs, too. To stay here and be part of this bustling family community is a privilege. If we were to derive our view of modern England from newspapers alone we would be sadly unaware that farming families such as this not only stay together and help each other out but thrive.

Henry and Enid were both Young Farmers – a solid rural beginning. They met at a car rally. Henry was working on this farm and Enid was working with her father, a butcher who also farmed. In fact, her family's farming story began even earlier than Henry's. But she moved in with Henry, into a bungalow built for them on the farm; when his parents retired, they moved into the main house.

They had three sons: Duncan, who now looks after the sheep, Angus, who cares for the cattle, and Henry, who works in London in the world of finance. He was headed that way long ago, while the other two were bent on farming. So Henry was given a private education to equip him for London, with the B&B providing the fees. (The Tourist Authority soon provided three stars – and an insistence on trouser presses, unused to this day.) Duncan went to Kirby Agricultural College and met Zoe there, a Newcastle girl happy to roll sleeves up and help out with the B&B. Janice was lured to the farm by Angus's inability to leave it, so busy was he; she stayed to help out and is now full-time. Enid talks of these girls as 'hand-picked' and clearly rejoices in their

company. Laughter can often be heard in the kitchen, a charming surprise to those of us familiar with the language of the modern chef.

With encouragement from their vet, Angus and Duncan have converted the farm to organic methods – the beginning of what should be a long but satisfying, and profitable, journey. Hand in hand with this goes an appreciation of good food and there is

"Zoe works an old-fashioned magic in the kitchen"

no shortage of local suppliers. Best of them all is David Carr, whose fabulous little village shop in Longframlington won the Countryside Alliance's 'Best Rural Retailer of the North East' in 2006. There are Craster kippers, local cheeses, and vegetables; David rises before dawn four days a week to buy them. The shop is the heart of the community and David, there since the 1970s, is much loved and respected. "If I haven't got something I'll get it. Things are much better than they used to be for local suppliers." The 'girls' at Thistleyhaugh are some of the suppliers' biggest fans and his best customers.

It is entirely possible, of course, for good food to be ruined once it hits the kitchen. But Zoe works an old-fashioned magic with it. For dinner, after a convivial sherry in the Garden Room or under the arbour watching the setting sun, you could be treated to courgette and roule cheese soup, Thistleyhaugh roast chicken and a fruit-studded pavlova. Dinner is around the big table, all guests joining the conversation; some enjoy themselves so much they arrange to meet here again, year after year. Breakfasts, too, are sumptuous. It's a handsome and comfortable Georgian farmhouse, and an easy place to mix with others. Enid is a relaxed hostess. If it's wet, you can stay all day. "People ask if they have to dress for dinner. I laugh and tell them that, well, they need to put something on!"

The five guest rooms are awash with space, old paintings, crisp linen, bits and pieces of fine old furniture and peaceful views over the garden and the

farm beyond. There are, generously, two sitting rooms for guests, with open fires, books galore and some of Enid's art collection, put together with income from her B&B. Step beyond the 700 acres and there are the Cheviots to discover. The village of Hartburn is built dramatically high above the Hart – the burn on one side, a stream on the other – and Mitford, the village of the Mitford family, is set in a wooded valley and still somehow removed from this century.

The family has always considered itself a guardian of the countryside, a far cry from the agricultural barons of East Anglia for whom land is a business asset. It is good to remember that farmers have the Herculean task of keeping England looking beautiful for us all. If they were properly rewarded for that they wouldn't have to struggle so hard to keep heads above water. However, farming remains tough, so the role played by visitors to the B&B has been crucial in giving the family the extra security needed. In return, they show a natural warmth towards visitors. "People often arrive stressed and after their second glass of wine at dinner they open up. By the time they leave they are changed people. They unravel."

The fact that the family thrives so well, working and living seven days a week under the same roof, must have much to do with this unravelling. It is interesting to reflect that many of us appear to believe that the only way for families to stay together is to live apart.

Henry & Enid Nelless

Thistleyhaugh,
Longhorsley, Morpeth, NE65 8RG
- 5 rooms.
- £80. Singles £55-£75.
- Dinner £20.
- 01665 570629
- www.thistleyhaugh.co.uk
- Train station: Alnmouth or Morpeth

West Coates

NORTHUMBERLAND

Three miles from the Scottish English border, old Berwick-upon-Tweed has changed hands fourteen times: more than any other border town. As a result, its character is a lovely balance of both England and Scotland, while the town walls, built and rebuilt many times, are among the finest examples anywhere of Elizabethan defences.

Karen's house is a ten-minute walk from the town centre – along the river, past three bridges – so you have the best of both worlds: country and town. For the country lover there is a beautiful coastline, and, of course, the whole of Northumberland. For the eco-aware there is a sense of being in a house that works hard to do the right thing. For the food lover there are the sea and the land, and fine local producers.

Langoustines fresh from the sea, split and grilled with garlic and herb butter; griddled sea bass, equally fresh and local, and roasted peppers stuffed with tomatoes and anchovies; broccoli and potatoes from the garden. Then, to ensure your return, strawberry ice cream with soft fruits from the garden and locally made organic meringues. Karen's cooking is irresistible – or so our readers tell us – and her sourcing of ingredients impeccable. Robson & Son provide Craster kippers, arguably the best in the world; the ice cream is Doddington's. Karen even runs cookery classes, small, laid-back,

low-key, for adults and children in the autumn and winter. If you ever wanted to expand your repertoire of recipes with spectacular dishes while appearing calm and completely in control, here's how.

Lindisfarne is just to the south, on Holy Island, a name that conjures more magic than most in England. The island is soaked in history and meaning, and is only thirty minutes from Berwick by bus, or twenty minutes by car. The island's oysters are among Britain's best, too.

Karen was brought up in the hills, twenty miles away. "My father was a proper shepherd and Mum helped on the farm." Karen met Logan when she was sixteen and married him at twenty-two. They bought a run-down farm at Jedburgh where, for ten years, Karen looked after its day to day running. It was a beautiful place, with water only from springs, but they loved it.

Then they sold up. One day, strolling through Berwick, they saw this house for sale and fell for it. It was solidly built by a merchant in the 1870s and needed little more than redecorating; bright glossy walls were repainted, brown carpeting whipped away. They have been determined to keep the atmosphere of a big traditional family home, with good furniture, relaxed spaces and very fine bathrooms. Now three elegant bedrooms with fruit, homemade

cakes and fresh flowers welcome you. "The house cried out to be used as a B&B."

Their purposeful recycling allows them to put out rubbish only once every two weeks – impressive

> "The organic eggs are particularly good, and make a lemon curd that has won awards"

for a house with three guest bedrooms. "It's all about organising yourself, avoiding packaging, asking people what they want to eat so you don't waste food," says Karen. "We do it our way and enjoy it. We have always used local suppliers; local food is part of my life, the way I was brought up."

Logan is in the livestock industry and is passionate about the quality of the local lamb and beef. The best quality Aberdeen Angus beef comes from neighbours who farm Castlehills and run the Well Hung & Tender meat company. (Karen often serves fillet steak, sometimes with a luscious madeira sauce.) The organic eggs are particularly good, and make a lemon curd that has won awards – and an army of fans – for Karen.

Karen's background was in the hotel and catering business, having qualified in this in Edinburgh. The children, both at university, Angus in Leeds and Isla in Aberdeen, are very happy to help out when required. The large leafy garden, full of interesting places to sit and read, is a haven for wildlife, especially birds.

L S Lowry was fond of Berwick, visiting many times from the mid-1930s to 1975. He did more than thirty paintings and drawings here and came the year before he died. The crisp, clean air was an antidote to the polluted city and he loved drifting among the back streets. There is a Lowry Trail now. Beyond the town is a coastline of ravishing beauty, and the bird-rich Farne Islands to the south. Bamburgh's castle is one of the country's most impressive, dominating the coast from its great

basalt outcrop. The village of Craster is rugged and delightful; at the turn of the century it had twenty boats supplying four kipper and herring yards. Now there is only one, but at least it survives. Alnwick Gardens is just a bus ride away. Hikers can plunge into the county's interior while urbanites can hop onto the Edinburgh to Newcastle train - the journey is interesting as much of the railway hugs the coast.

Karen and Logan are among the happiest of people, and one can see why. They have found a way of life that suits them. "We enjoy meeting the people that come through the door. We hardly ever do one nights. People come to completely wind down, and to explore Northumberland." As one guest tells us, "the whole family seems to get involved in making one's stay memorable." All who arrive stressed leave revived.

One couple were, perhaps, a touch too relaxed. "They were tired, also very laid-back, and they came down late to breakfast in their pyjamas. And did it again the next day!"

Karen Brown

West Coates,
30 Castle Terrace, Berwick-upon-Tweed, TD15 1NZ
- 3 rooms. £90-£120. Singles from £60.
- Dinner £35.
- 01289 309666
- www.westcoates.co.uk
- Train station: Berwick-upon-Tweed

Monmouthshire   Pembrokeshire   Ceredigion

Carmarthenshire   Conwy   Anglesey

WALES

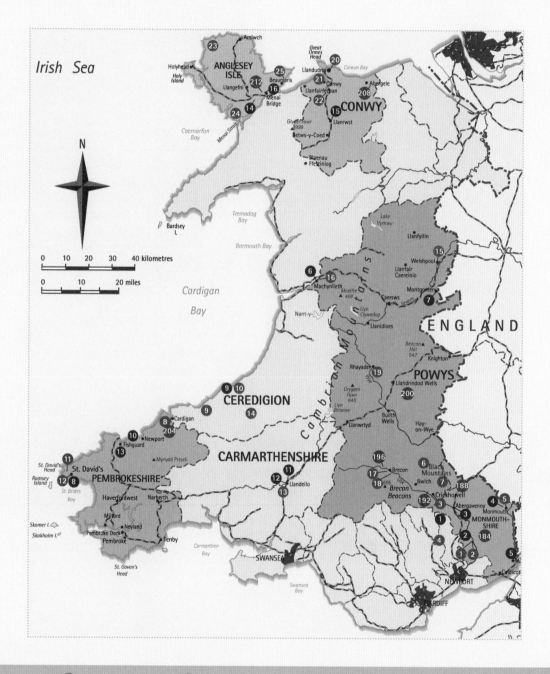

1 Slow travel   1 Slow food   1 Special places to stay (with page numbers)

WALES

Slow travel

1. Usk Castle
2. Usk Valley Walk
3. Glanusk Estate
4. Blaengawney Cider
5. Monmouth
6. Black Mountains
7. Llanthony Riding and Trekking
8. Welsh Wildlife Centre
9. Penbryn Beach
10. Llanerchaeron
11. St David's Head Walk
12. St David's Cathedral
13. Llandeilo
14. Llanybydder Livestock Market
15. Powis Castle & Garden
16. Centre for Alternative Technology
17. Brecon Beacons National Park
18. Cantref Pony Trekking
19. Elan Valley
20. Great Orme
21. Conwy Mountains Walk
22. Bodnant Garden
23. Melin Llynnon
24. Llanddwyn Island
25. Penmon Priory

Slow food

1. The Chef's Room Blaenavon
2. The Foxhunter
3. Abergavenny Food Festival
4. Ancre Hill Vineyard
5. Meadow Farm Tintern
6. Blasau Delicatessen
7. Castle Kitchen
8. St David's Food & Wine
9. Mariner Café
10. Wholefoods of Newport
11. Barita Delicatessen
12. Heavenly
13. Something's Cooking
14. Hooton's Homegrown
15. Blas ar Fwyd
16. Anglesey's Farm Foods

Special places to stay (with page numbers)

Slow travel

1 Usk Castle
Usk (01291 672563)
A castle in private hands, with crumbling stone walls and an inner bailey as unexpected as the Secret Garden, inhabited by hens, geese and the odd sheep. No fee: place a stone in a bowl to register your visit. Then amble down via the old railway into the town. Lovely.
www.uskcastle.com

2 Usk Valley Walk
One of the most gorgeous stretches of this 48-mile route from Brecon down to Caerleon and the sea is along the fish-rich river bank between Usk and Abergavenny. Every bit as pretty as the Wye.
www.uskvalleywalk.org.uk

3 Glanusk Estate
Crickhowell (01873 810414)
Luscious rolling acres, Celtic standing stones, a bridge over the River Usk, a private chapel, farm buildings and stables, 120 different species of oak, opera, agricultural shows and the Green Man Festival in August.
www.glanuskestate.com

4 Blaengawney Cider
Hafodyrynys (01494 244691)
Cider making days Sept to Dec and scrumptious scrumpy from Andy's homemade hand press - from sweet National Treasure to super-dry Heartbreaker. No chemicals, no sugars, no water, just apples.
www.blaengawneycider.co.uk

5 Monmouth
Tramp across the medieval Monnow Bridge and up the gentle high street to Agincourt Square. Antique and bric-a-brac shops abound.

6 Black Mountains
Haul yourself up to the blowy top of the Sugar Loaf (598m), through bucolically peaceful countryside sprinkled with fat sheep.

7 Llanthony Riding and Trekking
Llanthony (01873 890359)
The riding centre, based at Court Farm, lies in the shadow of the ruins of the 12th-century abbey, in the middle of the Brecon Beacons National Park. Saddle up and make for the moors where shaggy ponies roam. Dress up warm.
www.llanthony.co.uk

8 Welsh Wildlife Centre
Cilgerran (01239 621212)
Within the Teifi Marshes Nature Reserve, a contemporary glass visitor centre with panoramic views. Guided walks, adventure playground, balcony café, birds, butterflies, bats, bugs, fungi and frogs.
www.welshwildlife.org

9 Penbryn Beach
The most unspoilt beach on the Ceredigion coast, a mile of sands, dolphins, birdlife and seals (no dogs in summer). National Trust summer café on the hill, and footpath down to the beach via a wooded valley dappled with wood anemones in spring. Walk to Llangrannog past Morfa Cove - or, at low tide, to Tresaith.

10 Llanerchaeron
Ciliau Aeron (01545 570200)
An 18th-century self-sufficient Welsh estate: courtyard comes with dairy, laundry, brewery and salting house. Atmospheric walled gardens - in autumn, buy armfuls of old-species apples - pleasure grounds, ornamental lake and organically reared livestock.
www.nationaltrust.org.uk

11 St David's Head Walk
Circular three-hour walk from the golden sands of Whitesands Bay, taking in the wind-buffeted coastal path. Thrill to the Hats and Barrels - the rocks and reefs that still pose a threat to boats passing through these tidal races.
www.walkingworld.com

12 St David's Cathedral
In St David's, Britain's tiniest city, this imperious cathedral is tucked in a hollow beside the river. On the other bank is the Bishop's Palace, built in the 1300s, now an atmospheric ruin in which Shakespeare's plays are performed on summer nights. (bookings 01348 837034).

13 Llandeilo
Lovely shopping in lovely Llandeilo. Up streets of pastel-painted Georgian houses are little shops full of things you won't find anywhere else. Then climb up through Castle

Woods to Dinefwr Castle, perched on a high crag overlooking valley and river.

14 Llanybydder Livestock Market
A pungent mix of ewes, rams, cattle, tweeds, barbours and green wellies. Auctions on Fridays and Saturdays – check for dates. On the last Thursday of each month is Llanybydder's famous horse fair: who could resist a pretty Welsh cob?
www.evansbros.co.uk

15 Powis Castle & Garden
Welshpool (01938 551944)
High above Welshpool, with the vast castle as backdrop and views over the Severn, steeply sloping baroque terraces, billowing borders, astonishing topiary. Plus aviary, orangery and lead statuary.
www.nationaltrust.org.uk

16 Centre for Alternative Technology
Machynlleth (01654 705950)
In a woodland setting, the world-famous CAT. A water-powered funicular railway ferries you up to every eco technology under the sun, from solar thermals and wind turbines to compost loos and vast woodchip boilers. All this and coppicing skills.
www.cat.org.uk

17 Brecon Beacons National Park
The Brecon Beacons and Black Mountains teem with wildlife and breathtaking views, while the Visitor Centre outside Brecon has all the info, from family-friendly walks to national navigation courses, and all-year trips on the mountain railway.
www.breconbeacons.org

18 Cantref Pony Trekking
Cantref (01874 665 223)
Drop in to the longest established riding centre in Brecon for magic mountains, fairy-tale forests and plashing waterfalls. All ages from four.
www.cantref.com

19 Elan Valley
Northwest from Rhayader into wilderness and Devil's Bridge, and some of the remotest hiking south of the Cairngorms. Miles of peaty plateaus, a few sheep, wheeling kites, and five larch-lapped Victorian reservoirs with associated viaducts and dams. The 'Lakeland of Wales'.

20 Great Orme
Spot cashmere goats on wild grasslands as you board the Victorian funicular railway from Llandudno to the summit. Amble back through Haulfre Gardens, stop off at the Tea Rooms, drop down into the old town.
www.greatormetramway.co.uk

21 Conwy Mountains Walk
Starting point: SH778777: a superb five-mile circuit around the hills of Conwy Mountain with walking as adventurous as anywhere in Snowdonia - on a smaller scale. Details from Kinmel Arms page 208.

22 Bodnant Garden
Tal y Cafn (01492 650460)
Vast and beautiful gardens famous for laburnum walk (May/June), acres of camellias, magnolias and rhododendrons (April/May), and berrying autumn trees. Great views of Snowdonia.
www.bodnantgarden.co.uk

23 Melin Llynnon
Llanddeusant (01407 730797)
New wind farms stand in striking contrast to Anglesey's derelict flour mills. This one (1775) is the only working windmill in Wales. Summer tours, reconstructed round houses, tea shop and crafts.
www.visitanglesey.co.uk

24 Llanddwyn Island
Attached to the mainland at all but highest tides: a magical peninsula of wild grass-strewn dunes, rocky outcrops, exhilarating winds and safe swims.

25 Penmon Priory
Near historic Beaumaris, the ruins of a 13th-century monastery with carved arches, holy well and dovecot. The toll road leads to the viewpoint for a Victorian lighthouse and rocky Puffin Island.

Slow food

1 The Chef's Room Blaenavon
(01989 562353)
Cook it then eat it, with Slow Food writer Lindy Wildsmith and chef Franco Taruschio, founder of the legendary Walnut Tree. Morning courses for foodies, from summery seafood to autumn preserves.
www.thechefsroom.co.uk

2 The Foxhunter
Nantyderry (01873 881101)
Hunt and gather, then return to feast on samphire, sorrel, sea spinach, elderberries and nonfatal mushrooms. Enjoyable Slow food and rigorously seasonal produce.
www.thefoxhunter.com

3 Abergavenny Food Festival
Over a weekend in mid-September, the 'Glastonbury of food festivals'.
www.abergavennyfoodfestival.com

4 Ancre Hill Vineyard
Monmouth (01600 714152)
In a sunny limestone pocket of the Wye Valley, a tiny producer of pinot noir and an award-winning Chablis-like chardonnay. Lunch on Welsh cheeses, taste the wines, take a tour.
www.ancrehillestates.co.uk

5 Meadow Farm Tintern (01291 680 101)
Opposite the old railway station, beers from their brewery, preserves from their fruits, local apple juices and ciders, artisan cheeses... and willow weaving workshops.
www.meadowfarm.org.uk

6 Blasau Delicatessen
Machynlleth (01654 700410)
In the first capital of Wales, hand-finished olives, spicy bean pasties, single estate chocolates, charcuterie and champagne: all you need for a picnic sensation. Try before you buy, and sit down for a Welsh oggie and a coffee.

7 Castle Kitchen
Montgomery (01686 668 795)
Cute café, deli and restaurant in peaceful market town. Tuck into homemade hummus and local lemon sorbet on the terrace in summer. Buy a tranche of super-strength Montgomery cheddar.
www.castlekitchen.org

8 St David's Food & Wine
St David's (01437 721948)
People travel miles for the creamy Cenarth organic brie. Local bara brith too, meats, honeys, ciders, wines and scrumptious sandwiches for your picnic. In the café: laverbread, smoked Anglesey bacon, Snowdonia cheddar.

9 Mariner Café
New Quay (0545 560467)
A the bottom of the steep walk into New Quay, a salty spot for fish 'n' chips: perch on the ancient walls of the quay as seagulls wheel above – and land for rich pickings.

10 Wholefoods of Newport
Newport (01239 820773)
Vegetarian and vegan foods with a local and/or organic slant, plus a wholesome collection of books on the outdoors and all things green. Don't miss the Welsh honeys or the Celtic Crunch ice cream.

11 Barita Delicatessen
Llandeilo (01558 823 444)
In cute little Llandeilo, honey from Talley, Llanfaes ice cream, plaits of French garlic, laverbread pies, delicious Italian Illy coffee and walnut cake and organic home-baked bread.

12 Heavenly
Llandeilo (01558 822800)
Coconut mushrooms, buttered brazils, flambeed truffles, chocolate angels and marsala tiramisu ice cream from one of the naughtiest shops in Carmarthenshire.
www.heavenlychoc.co.uk

13 Something's Cooking
Letterston (01348 840621)
Cheap and cheerful, fresh and delicious: good people serving good fish 'n' chips... Rick Stein sings its praises.
www.somethingscooking.net

14 Hooton's Homegrown
Brynsiencyn, Anglesey
(01248 430344)
Free-range chicken, Welsh spring lamb, homegrown asparagus, strawberries, rhubarb, salads, spinach... The family farm bursts with picked-that-day produce. Pick your own from mid-June, feast your eyes on Snowdonia.
www.hootonshomegrown.com

15 Blas ar Fwyd
Heol yr Orsaf (01492 640215)
Little village deli packed with homemade pâtés, hunky hams, aged Welsh cheeses, interesting Welsh brews, wild mushrooms from locals, and a restaurant across the road.
www.blasarfwyd.com

16 Anglesey's Farm Foods
Sarn Fraint Farm, Penmynydd
(01248 712988)
Dynamic family-run organic farm. Angharad's butter is made from local cream and Halen Mon sea salt, jams from the hedgerows' blackberries and sloes; the bara brith is moist, light and fruity. Buy a hamper.
www.cynnyrchffermmon.com

Pubs & inns

Angel Inn

Salem, Carmarthenshire

Squishy sofas covered in throws, fairylights on corkscrew branches and a malty pint of Rev James: enjoy the quirky, homely charm. Divine food too in restaurant and bar, and portions hearty and satisfying. 01558 823394

Y Polyn

Nantgaredig, Carmarthenshire

A wicker sofa by the fire encourages you to loll, there's local art on bold walls, fresh flowers and candles. Chef-patrons Susan and Maryann know their onions, but you're just as welcome to pop in for a drink. 01267 290000

Harbourmaster Inn

Aberaeron, Ceredigion

Lobster boats at lunch, twinkling harbour lights at dinner, real ale, well-chosen wines and dazzling service. In the celebrated bistro, daily changing menus are studded with the best local produce. 01545 570755

Nag's Head Inn

Abercych, Pembrokeshire

Behind the orange exterior, a feast of pine and stone, and a chicken wire sideboard crammed with old bottles. Lots of quirkery, the heartiest of pub food, and a play area in the long lovely riverside garden. 01239 841200

Nantyffin Cider Mill Inn

Crickhowell, Powys

In the old drovers' inn are two intimate bars, and a high-raftered restaurant in the mill room. People pour in for flavoursome country cooking, ales and ciders on tap, punch in winter and homemade lemonade. 01873 810775

Bear Hotel

Crickhowell, Powys

This market-town inn hides a warm warren of surprises, and two dining areas for Welsh beef and salmon and sumptious puddings. At the back is a dog- and child-friendly garden. We've never seen the place empty. 01873 810408

Pen-y-Cae Inn

Pen-y-Cae, Powys

French windows open to the Brecon Beacons and all is pristine, from the multi-level garden to the claret leather sofas. Rib-eye steaks and laverbread pikelets are washed down with good bottled Welsh beers. 01639 730100

Ship Inn

Red Wharf Bay, Anglesey

The boatmen still walk across the estuary with their catch; tuck into turbot, crab, sandwiches, ales and Welsh cheeses from benches, pews and front terraces. Fires roar in several fireplaces in winter. 01248 852568

The Corn Mill

Llangollen, Denbighshire

A renovated corn mill by the swiftly flowing Dee, with a decked veranda over the rapids and an airy interior. Choose from a busy menu laced with contemporary ideas, watch dippers and wagtails as you sup. 01978 869555

Allt-y-bela

MONMOUTHSHIRE

There has always been a shy, secretive side to this beautiful building, hiding in its vivid-green valley. The writer and artist Fred J Hando describes a walk in the Monmouthshire countryside in search of Allt-y-bela in his 1951 book, 'Journeys In Gwent': "None of us had travelled this by-road before. As the lane wound this way and that, each small farm building brought forth the query 'Is this it?' The track became rough and rutted; the hills closed in on us; then as with one voice we ejaculated, 'Oh, there it is!' In a natural arena, shut away from the world, sheltered by wooded heights blue-green in the evening light, arose a group of grey buildings."

Allt-y-bela was first built as a hall house in the mid-fifteenth century. A traditional, single-storey cruck-frame building in which family and animals jostled for space and privacy was not expected. In 1599 a wealthy merchant Roger Edwards, probably having been inspired by tales of 'grand tours' and the resulting interest in architectural beauty, added a three-storey Renaissance tower – the first in Wales.

The fashion at the time, not surprisingly after all that proximity, was for light and space and for paring things back, perhaps mirroring the strive at this time for Puritanism among English Protestants. The tower has huge

rooms, each with windows on three sides – incredibly grand, and a novelty, at the time – and reminds us that when among architectural greatness less can be more.

The central staircase is circular and wooden and made from solid baulks of timber and may have been made by itinerant shipbuilders following the defeat of the Spanish Armada. There is a bell tower and a cider cellar and around this time cider production began in Monmouthshire.

For four hundred years the house, like the sleeping beauty, lay quietly. With very few changes of tenants there were hardly any alterations to its structure, which was a stroke of luck. But the years had taken their toll and by the 1980s, when Monmouthshire County Council was alerted to this architectural gem's parlous state, the wobbling tower was held together with makeshift scaffolding, water had seeped into the walls and the beams were infested with beetles. The Council served a compulsory purchase order and the rescue work began.

In stepped The Spitalfields Trust, a charity that dedicates itself to rescuing historically significant buildings, along with specialist architects and conservation builders. The Trust aims to repair rather than replace so all the internal timbers were treated and mended, fallen masonry was rebuilt and carefully replaced and blended

with surviving stonework, rotten beams were spliced with steel and mullioned windows restored.

By the time studded doors were added and the outside re-rendered in a cream lime plaster all that was needed was a buyer, so that once again Allt-y-bela could come alive.

William and Arne wanted to move West and had been looking for the right property for years. They saw this and were, unsurprisingly, smitten when they whizzed down to see it. They put in an offer the next day but it took time to sell their old house and there was an anxious year before Allt-y-bela was theirs. Arne says the wait wasn't a disaster: "It gave us a chance to absorb the landscape, the house and its grounds and the countryside."

It was in Arne and William's characters to want to share the magic of the reborn Allt-y-bela. Added to that, they both have a passion for good food and

> "There is deep comfort: house and water are heated with startling efficiency by a powerful log gasification boiler system fuelled by wood from coppicing in their own grounds"

are excellent cooks. All vegetables are home-grown, soft fruit in summer comes straight from the garden and your breakfast eggs will be supplied by the hens that roam freely through the flowers. Good suppliers are abundant in this valley, too: meat comes from Neil James the rare breeds butcher in Raglan, bread from Wigmore's bakery in Monmouth and fish from Usk where there is also a good farmers' market. William and Arne are generous souls who look after their guests with a light, easy touch. You can join them for supper in the kitchen, and are welcome to help with preparations.

You will sleep in one of two gloriously enormous bedrooms with beautiful, elegant pieces of original and period furniture, a huge oil painting here, a

stone sculpture there. Bathrooms are generous and beautiful with cast-iron tubs. It's striking and natural: the architecture doesn't need jewellery, and those who appreciate it will fall instantly under its spell. There is deep comfort: house and water are heated with startling efficiency by a powerful log gasification boiler system fuelled by wood from coppicing in their own grounds.

You will find space, privacy, quiet, a bucolic landscape and heaps of culture: castles at Raglan, Usk and Skenfrith and medieval churches (a must-see is the delicately-carved wooden rood screen at St Jerome's in Llangwm). Woodland walks and rambles over the hills would take up the rest of your time.

We can picture Roger Edwards on his horse, admiring his grand design once more and watching Allt-y-bela's own renaissance with approval. The trees are bouncing with birds, Hudson the cat patrols beneath, the dogs wait for their walk and William and Arne imbue the place with a quiet elegance.

William Collinson

Allt-y-bela,
Llangwm Ucha, Usk, NP15 1EZ
- 2 doubles
- £125.
- Farmhouse supper £30.
- 07892 403103
- www.alltybela.co.uk
- Train station: Newport

Court Farm

MONMOUTHSHIRE

Put your faith in the single-track road that cuts its way through the mountains of the remote Vale of Ewyas and leads all the way to the twelfth-century Llanthony Priory. A handful of stone farmhouses clings to the valley sides; Offa's Dyke is high up to your right; overhead, there might be buzzards, peregrine falcons, sparrow hawks or even a pair of red kites. As the track nears the Priory there is an exhilarating, palpable, sense of entering a sacred, untouched place.

The ruins of the Priory – known locally as 'the Abbey' – are majestic: built for Augustinian canons, it had a massive crossing tower and long arcaded aisles – elaborate in such a remote valley.

Throughout history the spectacular location has been the chosen home of a distinguished list of itinerants: St David, the patron saint of Wales, built a chapel here in the sixth century; Turner painted it in the summer of 1794; Walter Savage Landor the Victorian poet built his house here in 1806. Just eighty years ago the designer, sculptor and artist Eric Gill lived in the valley alongside other painters and engravers.

Following the patronage of Henry I the Priory expanded between 1174 and 1220, and there, as in every other priory, the monks made their own ale. It's a delight to discover that you can still drink beer there today: the twelfth-century

vaults of the Priory are now a Public House, and provide Colin's Sunday evening retreat.

Colin and Cordelia Passmore's farm butts on to the ruins and you stay in the former Prior's lodgings. Cordelia has carefully converted this medieval wing of the farmhouse into a two-bedroom guest suite.

A solid, oak-studded door leads into stone-flagged, thick-walled rooms resonating with medieval atmosphere; oak doors and furniture, flagstone floors, deep windows and log fires sit happily with the recently refurbished kitchen and bathroom; wild flowers spill out of vases, the chunky farmhouse table invites convivial eating and comfortable sofas surround the old iron range.

The main bedroom has a carved wooden bedhead and, beneath the weighty stone fireplace lintel, a seventeenth-century oak chest. The windows look out to the mountains on each side.

"I slowly make improvements," says Cordelia, "and try to keep the medieval feeling but add a little elegance." There is too, a quiet sense of grace and comfort.

The bathroom is accessed quirkily, as with many ancient buildings, through the kitchen, but what joy to slip into a roll-top bath next to an age-worn, pretty pine cupboard of fresh towels.

Colin's family has farmed at different locations in southern Britain for more than four centuries, but he feels especially blessed to have ended up in Llanthony. Even after years of living here the views can surprise him. "Walk across fields of sheep, through bluebell woods, up to the ridge two thousand feet above the valley floor, and huge sweeping landscapes greet you as you look over into England on the one side, Wales on the other. But I find my own special view walking down the fields at dusk, to the quiet of the Abbey below. The mood and presence of the ruins seem to change with the light, and the same happens to the hills above."

The 270-acre farm is home to six-hundred Welsh Mountain Cross sheep, sixty head of pedigree Hereford cattle (only Offa's Dyke separates them

> "I find my own special view walking down the fields at dusk, to the quiet of the Abbey. The mood and presence of the ruins seem to change with the light"

from their spiritual home), seventy-nine horses and ponies and one floppy eared bunny. Wild Welsh ponies roam the mountains.

Some of the lamb and beef ends up in the farm's cold room, where the well-hung meat is expertly butchered by Kris who has drawn inspiration from Hugh Fearnley-Whittingstall's courses at River Cottage; some ends up for sale at Cordelia's farmhouse door. "We're not registered organic, although we farm in an organic way," says Colin. Pork comes from the next valley and free-range eggs from a neighbour; there's a market garden, Peppe's, at the bottom of the valley and a Farmers' Market in Abergavenny. Add the vineyard on the southern slopes of Sugar Loaf Mountain and you have ensured your holiday is free from high street shopping.

Colin's son Tom runs the riding school and at times the yards are busy with activity when riders of all abilities are matched to horses; beginners are as

welcome as experienced riders, all eager to get out on to the open mountain where they can literally ride for miles.

Walking routes sweep past your oak-studded front door. Stride up onto Hatterall Hill, part of Offa's Dyke, or the Ffawddog ridge on the other side of the valley, teeter on the top with views of the Malvern Hills, the Welsh Black Mountains and the distinctive Sugar Loaf and Skirrid mountains.

Summer picnics amongst the purple heather are glorious and children can pootle very happily in the valley bottom amongst the 'dingles', the tiny streams, that run into the river; boating on the Brecon canal makes for a dreamy day.

The old drovers' tracks on each side of the valley are dotted with shepherds cottages, some inhabited, many not. As you climb beyond these, deep into the countryside, the sounds of the twenty-first century disappear, and you're left just with birdsong, the breeze and an ancient peace.

Cordelia & Colin Passmore

Court Farm,
Llanthony, Abergavenny, NP7 7NN
- Cottage for 4/5 £340-£500 p.w.
  Short winter breaks from £240.
- Self-catering.
- 01873 890359
- www.llanthonycourt.co.uk
- Train station: Abergavenny

Gliffaes Hotel

POWYS

It's the silence that hits you first, or rather the unsullied noise of nature. Deep in the Brecon Beacons National Park in South Wales, Gliffaes is a world away from the busy roads of our crowded lives among an ensemble of gently spreading trees and meadows.

"Spring is phenomenal here," says James. "The countryside is thick with wild cherry blossom, daffodils, snowdrops, bluebells. And the birdlife is amazing. We see red kites, buzzards and curlews; tawny owls set up home in the trees right outside the house." The fishing season starts in March and, as days grow longer and warmer, guests stay out late in the hope of catching brown trout or salmon gliding through the Usk's well-managed waters. Autumn brings pheasant and venison to the table and winter sees folk drawing up after frosty walks to the warmth of logs burning in the sitting room's beautifully carved fireplace.

In an age where impersonal chain hotels can seem to dominate, it is refreshing to come across a true family business. Susie's grandparents converted the grand Victorian manor house, a product of Wales' coal mining wealth, into a hotel shortly after World War II. Money was tight and tourism even less developed than today, but somehow it took off. They handed the hotel down to Susie's parents, who invited their daughter and James into the business in 1997. The couple enjoy working together – "not many people are lucky enough to spend all day with their husband or wife!" – and put in an enormous amount of energy, appearing at front of house six nights out of seven. "We want to pass this on to our daughters Alexandra and Olivia and are here for the long term. We plough as much as we can back into the building and the grounds."

With owners so closely involved day-to-day, guests are guaranteed personal attention. Susie's

father would tell fondly of an eccentric Admiral who arrived every year on the first of March and stayed until September, fishing every single day and insisting on rice pudding each lunchtime.

Food now comes from the kitchen of long-standing head chef Carl Cheetham who creates innovative menus from local, seasonal produce. "We grow our own salads, herbs, courgettes and beetroot and we have an apple orchard and keep chickens for eggs," says James whose new passion is his 'accelerated composter'. "We also forage for blueberries, blackberries, elderflowers and mushrooms. Sometimes I'll shoot a rabbit and it will go into a terrine." And if an angler lands a brace of trout or a salmon, he can have the pleasure of eating it that night.

As members of the Slow Food movement, James and Susie are passionate about sourcing good quality local food. Lamb and beef – excellent in this area, where traditional farming practices still predominate – come from Middlewood Farm, bacon and sausages from a butcher in Brecon, and in summer local organic vegetable growers deliver produce. One of their trusted sources is Penpont Estate's organic walled garden in Brecon (see next entry). Thay only serve Marine Stewardship

Council-approved fish. Says James: "It limits choice but we cannot continue to rape our seas. If people could see what was going on they would understand."

Down in the lovely Victorian cellar rest a hundred wines from around the world, including some promising English vintages. And although most

> "We could happily spend a week or more without leaving our grounds, except perhaps to cycle to Crickhowell"

guests stay for dinner every night, they're encouraged to try out some of the area's other good restaurants – several have Michelin stars.

There is no metronome. Life moves at its own relaxed rhythm, and guests slip in and out between fishing, golfing, bird-watching, hiking or simply sitting on the terrace, wine glass in hand, watching swifts and house martins swoop and, then, after the sun sets, darting bats. James recommends cycling as the best way to get around and can arrange bike

hire; he also keeps a tandem. "If you only see the countryside from your car, windows shut and air conditioning on, you filter out most of what is so special about the landscape," he says.

The nearest village is Crickhowell, a lively community with several pubs and cafés, a new brasserie, art shops and a tourist information office of which James is Director. Many of the volunteer staff have lived in this spot all their lives and, generous of spirit, are eager to help others discover its secrets.

The scenery ascends dramatically and culminates in the Black Mountains on the eastern side of the Brecon Beacons National Park, between Hay-on-Wye, Abergavenny and Crickhowell. The range emphasises the frontier between lowland England and highland Wales: a dramatic escarpment looks over tranquil English pastures to the east, and westward across spectacular ridges and steep remote valleys. James, who trained infantry soldiers at the army base in Brecon before meeting Susie – at the Gliffaes bar, by the way – knows the terrain well. "I spent two years running around the Brecon Beacons after Ghurkhas – they act as the enemy during army training sessions –

and have probably spent a hundred nights there out in the open."

James and Susie relish their life at Gliffaes: they enjoy the challenge of being able to turn their hand to anything and love living among so much beauty. "I have to be able to skin a rabbit, fix an oven and then appear dressed for dinner and recommend a wine to go with the Brecon lamb," says James. "We're privileged that we are able to spend a lot of time with our daughters. We could happily spend a week or more without leaving our grounds, except perhaps to cycle to Crickhowell. We love our life here and don't miss the bright lights at all."

Susie & James Suter

Gliffaes,
Gliffaes Road, Crickhowell, NP8 1RH
- 23 rooms.
- £99-£238.
- 3 course dinner £36.75.
- 01874 730371
- www.gliffaeshotel.com
- Train station: Abergavenny

Penpont

POWYS

Deep in the Brecon Beacons National Park, the entrance to Penpont gives nothing away. But drop down through Gavin's beloved woods, past the church and the soaring specimen trees, and you find lush lawns and a grand colonnade – pasted like a moustache onto a sober Georgian face. This is one aspect of Penpont, the Grade I-listed country house on the banks of the Usk. Go round into the cobbled, creeper-hung courtyard and meet the kindly face of the older, humbler farmhouse that spreads its labyrinth behind: the Courtyard Wing is the other aspect of Penpont, the friendly family-furnished rooms of the guest quarters. Davina and Gavin, the nicest people imaginable, drive the whole with intelligence, organised informality and a committed slow, green approach.

Penpont is a place for free spirits. Children love it: woods for building dens, lively river for fishing, bats under the bridge, natural football pitches and croquet lawns, hideaways galore; there is a palpable sense of fun, even in the topiary. "We are privileged to have the time and mind space to be able to turn a boring square hedge into a herd of elephants going down to the river." says Vina. "It's a gardening challenge, a reminder of the baby elephant we 'adopted', and it's fun. Like the Green Man maze, which is a celebration of a powerful

pagan myth and an appeal to everyone's imagination."

Davina inherited this extraordinary place and its two thousand acres from her Uncle and Aunt. Their income had come from timber and tenant farmers. Post-war recession and supermarkets killed the rhyme and reason for such big estates and Aunt Jo retreated to the old nursery leaving the rest of the house to sleep timelessly behind shutters. When she died, the grand reception rooms were a curator's dream with their Edwardian draperies and giant Chinese urns, Chippendale furniture, fine books and ancestral portraits – a "foster-child of silence and slow time" – until the Sotheby's sale.

When, after six months of "of course we must" / "don't even think about it", the Hoggs moved in, they found no furniture and one single book: Bleak House. Why did they take it on? "We had been tree surgeons in Bristol for eight years," says Gavin, "and we needed a change." He had trained as an arboriculturist and the hectares of woodland here were tempting – but daunting. "We thought and hesitated, until in June we came and played: the sun shone, we picnicked, had fun – and fell in love with the place.

"Then we realised just how much change we'd got: the practical implications sank in, we became tied to the land and nature's cycles, discovering what we needed to do to exist within this environment. There's no supermarket near here, no corner shop, so we had to provide for ourselves. We live, work and play Penpont and the maze, planted for the millennium, expresses our sense of belonging here."

The four-acre Victorian walled garden is an organically certified source of fruit, vegetables, herbs and flowers, a shining example of how to do it. "I run it with one full-time gardener, one part-timer and a rotovator," says Vina. "They had nineteen outside staff, including eight gardeners, in the old days... We operate a closed system: the soil is fed with home-grown green manure (mostly phaecelia, ryegrass, clovers and vetch), muck from our horses

> "Our ten-pitch camping site in the old rose garden is a low-key, minimum-rules set-up for families who are looking for the camping they used to know"

grazing chemical-free fields, our garden compost and that essential tenet of the organic faith, crop rotation. These are the basic principles that I've learned from our two organic gardeners; they have been wonderful teachers as well as gardeners." The garden feeds Penpont, Vina's farm shop, several gastropubs, the Brecon theatre and a veg box scheme.

"Our six tenant farmers thought we were crazy at the beginning. Organic meant hippy and totally unqualified to farm. We planted trees on perfectly good grazing land! But the younger generation are beginning to see the sense of it."

Gavin has planted 100,000 trees in their twenty years here. "Because I love trees," he says simply, "and because they will gain in value, as building, furniture and biomass resources, as oxygen factory and carbon sink – there's no doubt about that today." The massive wood-chip boiler provides all the heat for the estate, saving sixty-six tonnes of carbon emissions every year. "We close the Georgian shutters, too, a brilliant barrier against the cold. And

moreover..., the boiler room below the guest wing is ideal for drying wet coats and boots."

Gavin is proud that the regenerated woodland is healthier and now, under an environmental forestry scheme, he is getting an even better return on his investment by selling wood-chipping services and biomass fuel to other businesses. "I sell the right wood for the job: low-grade for burning, better quality for building or furniture, it's the only sustainable way to manage forests. There's a plan to build the world's biggest wood-chip power station in Wales using 100,000 tonnes a year of wood chips imported from Canada. It's big-business madness! We shouldn't use high-value timber for burning and we should grow our own, not ship it across the Atlantic."

Penpont's other recent eco-development has been the stables conversion. "Penpont is a glorious place for celebrations – parties, weddings, fêtes – but rather than becoming a wedding factory we want to have a year-round calendar of exhibitions, music, theatre and retreats, for locals as well as people from further away. We salvaged and re-used the original structural timbers, used traditional lime mortars and washes, insulated with Thermafleece (made by a company that gives Welsh hill farmers a decent price for fleeces). Those who have used it are happy with the easy, natural feel. And our ten-pitch camping site in the old rose garden is a low-key, minimum-rules set-up for families who are looking for the camping *au naturel* they used to know." Penpont is indeed a realm for free spirits and nature lovers.

Davina & Gavin Hogg

Penpont,
Brecon, LD3 8EU
- Courtyard wing sleeps 15-17 in 6 bedrooms.
- £1,450 per week; £850 short breakds
- Self-catering
- 01874 636202
- www.penpont.com
- Train station: Abergavenny

The Yat

POWYS

The Yat sits, sheltered, in a deep valley, in an area once known as Wild Wales. Although remote, it has many foreign connections: the Romans built a fort here in an attempt to keep the unruly Celts down and, later, St David set up a monastic community and converted those Celts to Christianity.

The ancient rambling Yat possibly dates from the fourteenth century, though its history may go back further. The house, once the local squire's residence, was the most important house in the hamlet and part of the Cwm Mawr estate. It is tucked away from harsh winds and surrounded by beautiful trees and hills whose colour changes with the seasons.

The history of the house and the tiny hamlet of Glascwm is evident in the stone whitewashed cottages and large thirteenth-century church. It was once on the drovers' route, but is now more of a peaceful backwater. The house and the setting fuels Krystyna's considerable creativity. Born of Polish émigré parents on a Welsh hill farm after the Second World War, she studied art at Chelsea and the Warsaw Academy of Fine Art. She worked in London but then came back to Wales with her husband, a Scot, who embraced the Celtic ethos. Krystyna had taught art and 'preached' ecology until she thought it was time to practise what she preached. "When we saw The Yat in all its timeless beauty we knew we had found our retreat."

The sixth-century monks chose the spot for its special energy and beauty and Krystyna, who ran art workshops here, sees the house as a kind of retreat, somewhere that still invites contemplation. Baptists arrived in the seventeenth century and made this their home; one minister gave a sermon from a high window to a hundred people gathered on the lawn and in the garden there remain the ruins of an old Baptistry and a private graveyard. The spring that gave water to the monks and the Baptists still gives water

today; sheep outnumber people; wild horses roam the hills, on which you can walk out and yell, or sing, to your heart's content and disturb no one.

The pictures painted in Dylan Thomas's hymn to his nature-bound childhood at his uncle's farm are still here:

> And then to awake, and the farm, like a
> wanderer white
> With the dew, come back, the cock on his
> shoulder: it was all
> Shining, it was Adam and maiden,
> The sky gathered again
> And the sun grew round that very day.
> So it must have been after the birth of the
> simple light
> In the first spinning place, the spellbound horses
> walking warm
> Out of the whinnying green stable
> On to the fields of praise.
>
> Fern Hill 1946

The sense of living with the past is vital to The Yat's atmosphere. "We are not owners but caretakers," says Krystyna. Strangers who lived here or visited come to the house and fill in gaps of the house's history. It has affected so many.

Krystyna and Derek renovated sensitively: wattle and daub was used instead of plaster, ancient beams uncovered and flagstones carefully lifted to install underfloor heating, then replaced. Woodburners, a condensing oil-fired burner and central heating give further warmth and solar panels heat the water.

A local blacksmith hand-made the wrought iron gate copying a seventeenth-century design of rambling vines. "I was allowed to make two of the leaves," says Krystyna, who also helped to design the free-standing kitchen with a local cabinetmaker. Oak was used in the kitchen, for the conservatory and for doors and windows. Leaded windows with, possibly, twelfth-century glass were carefully restored, as were the seventeenth-century window catches.

But the first thing Derek and Krystyna did on their eight-and-a-half-hilly acres was to plant a

thousand trees, most of them native deciduous species but with a few specimen trees added. In the twenty years the couple have owned The Yat not a drop of artificial fertiliser has touched the soil and the area is alive with songbirds. The ancient garden terraces have been extended; dry stone walls, steps, a small fountain and an ornamental pond have been added. "Ancient box hedges shelter those who want to rest or meditate," says Krystyna.

"Blackcurrants, gooseberries and plums grow and there is a terraced vegetable garden. We use our own organic vegetables and meat for the table whenever possible and buy meat from Craig Farm and beef from the farm on which I was born. We like guests to feel as if they are family friends and so they can, if they like, eat their meals with us. If we go to the Arts Centre in Builth Wells we might invite guests to share this outing with us." Guests can help themselves to tea and coffee in the dining room and maybe home-made biscuits or cakes.

Krystyna's spiritual sense of natural processes feeds her awareness of things religious and she is deeply aware of nature. She is currently nurturing a project in Poland to restore an empty, half derelict, classical manor house and turn it into a people's college for east-west cross-cultural education, also teaching eco friendly agricultural and crafts.

At The Yat, Krystyna and Derek plan to have a yurt and, perhaps, a tree house. A thoughtful couple, they are working for today and the longer term. In Krystyna's words, "We hope to create a place where there is unity between man, mind and nature, a homely place, yet full of life and joy."

Krystyna Zaremba

The Yat,
Glascwm, Llandrindod Wells, LD1 5SE
- 2 rooms. £75. Singles £55 (except during Hay Festival/Royal Welsh Show).
- Dinner, 3 courses, £30.
- 01982 570339
- www.theyat.net
- Train station: Builth Wells

fforest

PEMBROKESHIRE

The taste of freshly brewed coffee, mingled with the smell of dew. Birdsong at sunrise, crickets at dusk. A tapestry of wild meadows, fields and woodland enveloping lush rolling hills. The adrenalin of scaling cliffs, kayaking, climbing trees. The splash of the sea. The simple pleasure of cooking outdoors by a crackling fire. The knowledge that your impact on nature is minimal, your carbon footprint almost zero. The conviviality of it all...

Staying at fforest might technically be called camping, but if your childhood memories involve deflating air mattresses, stones under the groundsheet, cold baked beans, dripping tents and single gaz burners, this is a world away.

To appreciate how fforest has become an exceptionally special camping outfit in a beautiful remote corner of West Wales you must delve into the story of its creators James Lynch and Sian Tucker. "Creativity is in our blood," says James. "We've been involved with design, architecture, building and marketing all our lives. The concept evolved naturally, like a collage. First I bought this two-hundred-acre farm on an instinct. I had no commercial agenda and knew nothing about farming. It's ancient land. The estate belonged to the Royal Surgeon of Queen Anne, oddly, as it's a long way to court from here!"

James and Sian have artistic backgrounds: James attended Central Saint Martin's College of Art and Design; Sian studied textile design at the Royal College of Art. They and their boys, Calder, Robbie, Jack and Teifi, have settled happily in the country.

The land had gone slightly wild, giving the couple freedom to carve out spaces on a canvas of wilderness rather than deal with manicured hedges and fences. The original plan, inspired by a Norwegian artists' community James had visited twenty years ago, was to build eco-cabins using the abundant local Douglas fir, but the village community voted against it. "Even

MMEAL NIGHT
TUESDAY
SIGN UP IN OFFICE

in 2005, 'eco' was a scary word: it meant Swampy," says James. "Thankfully things have moved on."

This initial set-back encouraged a more innovative, lower-impact idea: bespoke tents with all the comforts and services of a hotel room yet a more elemental, communal experience. Guests come together for breakfast of local produce and for dinner prepared in the outdoors two nights a week, as well as during activities.

You can stay in a 'nomad', a Dutch-style tunnel tent with two sleeping pods; or a huge 'dome' tent with solid wood floor and bay window; or a 'bell' tent, open-plan with a wood-burner; or a 'threepi', based on a Swedish kåta but with a suspended wood-burner and domed rooflight. Some have king-size beds and duvets, others reindeer hides and Welsh woollen blankets, woven to Sian's designs in a 200-year-old-mill in nearby Dre-fach Felindre, part of Wales' National Wool Museum. And for those who must have their comforts, there are 'croglofts', stone cottages with soft beds, private bathrooms, underfloor heating and wood-burning stoves.

"I've ended up creating things I like, in a place I like, for people I like, with the people I love," says James. The couple spent thirty years in Shoreditch, London, developing workshops and apartments by day and holding notorious raves in their 3,000-square-foot basement, 'The Tinderbox', by night. "I loved London but I reached a stage where I wanted to feel rewarded in a different way. We considered moving to New Zealand but realised that West Wales, where the kids have played on the beach every summer throughout their lives, has pretty much everything New Zealand has. It was just that in the past Wales may have failed to market its fantastic natural assets in the same way."

fforest lies close to Cardigan by the River Teifi, an ice-age estuary carved out through the slate-rich land. During the nineteenth century the slate was quarried intensively and the debris tossed in the river, until one day quarrymen realised the waters had become too shallow for their barges.

It is now a rich wildlife sanctuary teeming with wild red deer, rare long-eared bats, kingfishers,

buzzards, red kites and a thriving otter community feeding on the masses of salmon and sewin (sea trout) who come here to spawn. Guests can explore by kayak or canoe or, when water levels rise, by raft. The most ancient vessel is a coracle, a simple bowl-shaped willow frame covered with canvas and tar. Coracles are an integral part of the local heritage: a small number of licences exist for 'coracle men', who pass both licence and skills down from father to son.

An important aspect of the experience is food; gardener Alice is developing a vegetable plot which produces veg for the shop. James can also demonstrate how to skin and joint game. "It makes people's eyes pop out of their heads," he says

You can learn to build natural shelters and camp fires without matches, or crafts such as green woodworking, coppicing and willow weaving. There's watery fun to be had, too, of course, and it is one of the pleasures of fforest that you can warm up afterwards in a cedar wood sauna and end the day with a drink in front of a roaring wood-burner.

Sian Tucker & James Lynch

fforest, fforest Farm, Cilgerran, SA43 2TB
- From £200 for 3 nights in a nomad to £1020 per summer week in a crogloft.
- Breakfast included; 2-course evening meal, £16, available 2 nights a week.
- 01239 623633
- www.coldatnight.co.uk
- Train station: Carmarthen/Aberystwyth

The Kinmel Arms

CONWY

On a crisp, clear Valentine's morning in 2002, Tim and Lynn bought each other a present that changed their lives: a former seventeenth-century coaching inn, tucked away in a tiny village near the North Wales coast. They both had childhood memories of the place as their families, from the same town but strangers to one another, used to frequent the pub. It wasn't until years later that the couple met, married and decided to return to their roots with their young son, Tom, to start a new branch of family history.

Gradually, and with over ten years of commitment, hard work and imagination, they have built up a deliciously peaceful place to eat, rest, sleep and explore.

The inn – warm stone walls punctuated by a parade of mullioned windows and topped by a racing green gable, the whole ensemble cocooned in a canopy of leafy trees – is remarkable on many counts but primarily for the food. "I don't like to put a label on our style of food," insists Lynn. "These are our creations." Menus are based around the seasons and on the ideas of Welsh chef Gwyn Roberts, who has come back to his homeland after a spell in London's top restaurants: you may find Welsh pancakes with gravadlax, roast monkfish tail wrapped in Carmarthen cured ham and a broad bean, shrimp and cockle sauce; mussels from the Menai Strait infused with orange, parsley, garlic and whisky, or braised venison from the nearby Kinmel Estate.

This book celebrates not just good food but good ingredients, and it is reassuring that the family grow and rear a good deal of these. A flock of hens produce all the eggs while pigs – Pietrin Welsh cross and a Wild Boar cross at the moment – gobble up leftovers and peelings. Their own lambs, looked after by a neighbouring farmer, appear on the menu, too. Tim likes to experiment in the Kinmel Arms vegetable garden, and his polytunnels are brimful with an array of exotic salads and brassicas including misuna, sorrel, komatsuna and pe-tsai.

The Kinmel Arms
St George

Restaurant with rooms

01745 832207

www.thekinmelarms.co.uk

Most other supplies come from the coast, just a few miles away, and the rich agricultural land of the Conwy Valley. Irrigated by the wide Conwy River, which shoots down from the high moorland of Central Snowdonia and spills out into the Irish Sea at Conwy Bay, this mineral-rich mining area supports abundant livestock. A pre-prandial stroll along Tim's Kinmel Arms Trail will take you past fields of Welsh Black, Charolais, Limousin and Highland cows, Beulah Speckled Face sheep and lambs, and Gloucester Old Spots, Saddlebacks and Large Whites. New organic cheeses such as the creamy blue Perl Lâs and fresh, brie-like Perl Wen from Caws Cenarth come from nearby farms. Llandudno's smokery provides haddock, peppered mackerel, trout and duck smoked over real Welsh oak.

The bar keeps ciders, beers and ales from local microbreweries with wonderfully evocative names like Snowdonia Ale from the Mŵs Piws (Purple Moose) Brewery and Landslide from Facer's Flintshire. The wine list does span the globe but there are some local Welsh varieties, too, such as the Penarth sparkling rosé or pinot chardonnay.

St. George – Llansan Siôr to its many Welsh-speaking residents – is a tiny nugget of tranquillity with just twenty-five families, a village school and a lively community that comes together for annual flower shows and pantomimes. This is walking country and for those who like to balance indulgence with activity Tim and Lynn provide maps, guides and leaflets. You can shadow the coastline along sections of the North Wales Path, ramble through bluebell woods alive with birds and roe deer, hike up Tower Hill for a view across the Great Orme and the mountains of Snowdon. Cyclists can follow the off-road North Wales Coastal Cycleway from Kinmel Bay through Rhos-on-Sea and Llandudno.

Tim and Lynn realised that to let the peace and beauty of the region sink in you need longer than a lunchtime and added four fine bedrooms at the rear. The walls are arm-length thick walls and hefty insulation and soundproofing were added along with new floors. Leaving the buzz of the restaurant behind, you slide into a bubble of serenity. The rooms – Driftwood, Pebble, Grace and Eryr – have ceilings spiked with skylights, super-king size beds handmade locally in oak and maple, porcelain bathrooms lined with travertine tiles and quartzite floors. Tim's paintings and photographs line the walls.

Breakfast can be taken at your leisure on the balcony that is hewn from Welsh green oak and faces east to catch the morning sun. Each room has a fridge packed with continental goodies: baked hams, local cheeses, homemade breads and Rachel's organic yoghurts (she lived locally before becoming famous), and there's a percolator for real coffee.

Tim, a primary school teacher as well as an artist and marathon runner, and Lynn, a business manager and fireball of energy, take pleasure in helping guests relax. Their commitment to their family, restaurant, guests, garden and animals is incredibly strong, and it is that commitment which should be championed as a path to success and a truly satisfying life.

Lynn Cunnah-Watson & Tim Watson

The Kinmel Arms,
The Village, St George, Abergele, LL22 9BP
- 4 suites.
- £115-£175.
- Dinner, 3 courses, £25-£30.
- 01745 832207
- www.thekinmelarms.co.uk
- Train station: Abergele-Pensarn

Neuadd Lwyd

ANGLESEY

Even the carefully sprinkled sea salt crystals on Susannah Woods' gourmet dinners are from Anglesey. For she and husband Peter are as passionate about their island as they are about history, gardening and good food – and the fewer the food miles the better.

There is a hierarchy in the Neuadd Lwyd (pronounced Nay-ath Lewid) kitchen. First come herbs, salads and vegetables from Susannah's organic kitchen garden and eggs from her hens. Then come fish and seafood – Atlantic mackerel, sea bass, lobsters, crabs – from Anglesey's harbours at Cemaes and Amlwch, and oysters from the Menai Strait. Meat comes from Welsh-breed cows and lambs reared on the island, while local dairy farms have started experimenting with cheeses: blue cheeses, soft cheeses, and five types of goat's cheese are all produced nearby. And if Anglesey cannot provide what she needs, then Susannah will seek it in mainland Wales, preferably within a thirty-mile radius.

Susannah's skill as a chef, combined with her passion for local, seasonal produce and her horror of anything tinned or pre-prepared – about the only thing that comes out of a packet is Llandudno smoked fish – result in an incredible gourmet experience. In the elegant dining room, tables are laid for dinner while Peter serves drinks with canapés in the drawing room before a blazing fire in winter or out on the terrace in summer. Locals can book in for dinner if the tables are not taken by guests, and the atmosphere is buzzy, refined and full of anticipation.

Four-course menus change daily in line with what's fresh and according to Susannah's fertile imagination. Spelt risotto with Cemaes Bay crab and garden leeks could be followed by slow Aga-cooked Anglesey lamb shank and cônfit of shallot and thyme in a rosemary and red wine jus. For dessert, try

lavender-scented panna cotta with home-grown berry compôte, then a plate of local cheeses. Handmade petit fours accompany coffee.

"We feel it is so important to give guests a sense of place," Susannah emphasises, "to give them a taste not only of our food but of our heritage." Susannah is a native Welsh speaker and has created an environment that is refreshing for Welsh guests and a cultural experience for others. Menus, wine lists and information booklets are bilingual and staff flip easily between both languages. You can request a pronunciation of the name of the nearby town Llanfairpwllgwyngyllgogerychwyrndrobwllllantysilio gogogoch (shortened, thoughtfully, to Llanfair PG). Welsh is one of the few minority languages in the world that are growing in popularity as regional cultural identity grows. Indeed, around seventy per cent of Anglesey's residents are Welsh-speaking.

The fact that Anglesey, or Ynys Môn in Welsh, is an island, helps deepen the sense of community here yet further. A sliver of sea, the Menai Strait, separates the island's two-hundred-and-eighty or so square miles from the North Wales mainland, with much of the coastline a designated Area of Outstanding Natural Beauty. Some say it is where you experience the best of Wales: coastal towns are linked by craggy cliffs, small bays and a one-hundred-and-twenty-five-mile signed walking path while, inland, foodies will discover a tight-knit network of local small producers and family farms. Susannah and Peter know them all, and have recently joined with Anglesey's Halen Môn Sea Salt company to found a Slow Food convivium to promote local produce.

The tiny hamlet of Penmynydd, which Neuadd Lwyd shares with just a few other families, is bound together by a rich history: the family which gave rise to Tudor royalty, including King Henry VIII and Queen Elizabeth I, lived and died here. Its graves lie in the tiny, ancient Church of Saint Gredifael just beyond the garden gate, where Susannah and Peter still worship and which they help to maintain with proceeds from afternoon teas and plant sales. (Neuadd Lwyd was the rectory until thirty-five years ago.) Anglesey has been

ruled and raided by Celts, Romans, the Irish, Vikings, and of course by the English; there is no end to stories and fascinating archaeological sites.

It was the history of the place that intrigued Susannah and Peter when in 2002 they decided to change their lifestyle. Susannah, a midwife, left the NHS and took a three-month course at Ballymaloe Cookery School in Ireland; Peter, a psychologist, cut down to a three-day week. It took the couple three years to renovate the time-worn building, installing en-suite bathrooms in the high-ceilinged rooms and creating the quintessential country house that they dreamed of owning. It has all been done with the utmost sensitivity and the aim of preserving the house's history and heritage. Bedrooms are named after members of the Tudor family and are filled with finely upholstered armchairs around original, ornate marble and slate fireplaces, while antique mirrors reflect iron-framed beds dressed in fine linen.

As such strong advocates for the island, Peter or Susannah will point you to the best sections of the coastal path, to the beaches of Llanddwyn and Red Wharf Bay and to nature reserves at Pentraeth and Newborough; to historic Beaumaris and the National Trust-run home of Lord and Lady Anglesey at Plas Newydd. To the south, parading past the drawing room, dining room and the front bedrooms, a spectacular view of the mountains of Snowdonia tempt walkers across to mainland Wales.

However you spend the day you return to elegant bedrooms, a soak in a slipper tub, a stroll in the garden, a book by the fire and whichever culinary extravaganza is destined for the table that night.

Susannah & Peter Woods

Neuadd Lwyd,
Penmynydd, Llanfairpwllgwyngyll, LL61 5BX
- 4 rooms.
- £125-£195 with full-Welsh breakfast.
- 4-course dinner £42.
- 01248 715005
- www.neuaddlwyd.co.uk
- Train station: Bangor

Soil Association

STUFFED*

POSITIVE GLOBAL ACTION FOOD CRISIS

Pat Thomas

featuring essays by
Michael Pollan, Geetie Singh, Monty Don, Rob Hopkins, Jeanette Orrey
Carolyn Steel, Peter Melchett, Vandana Shiva and Eric Schlosser

ecotricity

Thank you to Jeanette Orrey for her
permission to publish this extract from
her essay that appears in 'Stuffed'
(Sawday's Fragile Earth series, £14.99)
www.sawdays.co.uk/bookshop

*"My hope for the future is
that every child can sit
down at school and enjoy
a good, wholesome lunch
knowing where their food
has come from, and that
the catering staff are
given recognition."*

Transforming food culture in schools

Jeanette Orrey, a dinner lady for twenty years, pioneered the introduction of fresh, local and organic school meals. Her achievements and guidance led to the success of the Food for Life Partnership campaign and inspired Jamie Oliver's fight to improve school meals

It all started when I was the catering manager at St Peter's Primary School in Nottinghamshire. I was employed by the Local Authority, which had introduced Thatcher's recommendations for 'best value' for school meals. 'Best value' meant using the cheapest ingredients, taking away equipment and catering staff hours, and providing everything in boxes pre-prepared: carrots, onions, potatoes, coleslaw. I just couldn't believe that this was what we were serving to the children. None of the kitchen staff would eat it, including me. I knew something had to be done.

In 2000, with the head teacher's and governors' support, we decided to take the catering in-house. To begin with it was frightening as I knew I really had to make it work to prove that freshly prepared food was the way forward. I started by introducing local meat, then milk and then local and organic veg and potatoes. Meal numbers increased and it was a huge success with pupils and parents. In my quest to find new suppliers, I realised I could source local and organic produce directly from the growers at the same price as non-organic produce through a centralised wholesaler. What was important to me was that I could look the parents in the eye and tell them where the food I was serving their children came from. I just wanted to serve good, wholesome, honest food and it went down a treat.

While we had changed the food at St Peter's, we never thought about the bigger picture. It wasn't until I received a Soil Association award in 2002 and met Lizzie Vann (founder of Organix) that the real revolution began. People had been campaigning for better school meals long before I came onto the scene, but we were in the right place at the right time.

Lizzie and I then decided that we needed to roll this out and support more schools to do what we did at St Peter's. We took our 'Food for Life' idea to the Soil Association and set up a pilot scheme, which led to the Food for Life Partnership.

Part and parcel of this pilot scheme was a 'whole school approach' to food, which includes the dining experience. Many children don't eat at a dining table at home and social skills are lost. Using real cutlery and crockery and using tablecloths makes the dining hall into a dining room, where they can sit down and have the time to enjoy their food and socialise.

It's important to get schools cooking, growing and visiting farms, too, as one without the other doesn't work. Children need to know where the food they eat comes from in order to appreciate it.

I've asked children where potatoes come from and their answer was 'trees'. That worries me. St Peter's Primary School gets much of its produce from the local Gonalston Farm Shop, which also shows children how the sausages they eat at school are made, and to give them tastes of the local cheese. The children talk about the food they tried which inspires parents to go.

My hope for the future is that every child can sit down at school and enjoy a good, wholesome lunch knowing where their food has come from, and that the catering staff are given recognition. They play a crucial role in educating children about food.

We are moving in the right direction, but we are going to be under a lot of pressure in the next few years with the government cutting costs and the rise in food and oil prices. We only have one shot at this and we have to get it right. We owe it to future generations.

www.foodforlife.org.uk

Sawday's community garden

"Over fifty local people were waiting for an allotment so we set up our own growing project in the field next to our pigs and started digging," says Sawday's Nicola Crosse

Not since the forties has growing vegetables been so very much the 'in' thing. Celebrities shout about it, TV chefs show off their own patches and assure us it's all very easy, the National Trust has jumped on the bandwagon and even restaurant critic Giles Coren had a go at it. And quietly, 300,000 lucky allotment owners have just got on with doing it.

For me, it started with pigs and after discovering the merits of a pig-rearing group (sharing the feeding, tickling their tummies, cracking through the iced-up water troughs on dark January mornings, taking the trusting little things to slaughter) my thoughts started to turn towards what we could do with the rest of the field which was still largely unused.

I was keen on growing some veg. Even I had to admit it was far too big a project for one person, and then I discovered there were over fifty people in the village who were on the waiting list for an allotment. Bingo - the grower's group was born.

We had our first meeting in February '10. We're a mixed bunch: a homeopathic vet, a horticulturist (always useful), a couple of business people, two or three retired folk, a teacher, a civil servant, and an eager dog who barks a lot. It was agreed that some plots could be for individuals and the rest would be to share and our clever horticulturist got on with a beautifully-drawn plan. That was the easy bit.

Several decades of undisturbed couch grass was the first problem. We let the pigs have a go at it but, valiant as they were, they just couldn't dig up all that subterranean spaghetti. Two marvellous plough horses then had a go but their owner said it was like trying to plough coconut matting. So we hired a rotivator and Robert (our muscliest male) slaved away until it was done. Then came lovely spring sunshine, frantic planting and within a few short weeks onions, beetroot, potatoes, carrots, all sorts of beans, peas, courgettes and squashes were popping up and out all over the place.

A little shed went up, then a hammock, a swing, a Wendy house and a couple of benches. Children play, feed the chickens, chase the piglets and help pick the veg. The adults are behaving nicely, too, and so far there have been no quarrels about who has what. We weigh and record what we take to help with future planting plans.

Last night we had a chicken group meeting in the field and one of the piglets escaped and came and sat with us on the rug for a while, listening and watching as if she had an opinion to offer. I looked around me and saw all the lovely vegetables, and the chickens taking dust baths and making that comforting sound they make. A community allotment is far more than just somewhere to grow vegetables; it has brought very different people together and given us all a plentiful supply of good fresh produce. It's excellent exercise too!

"Having animals and a community farm next to our office means even I'm getting in touch with my inner farmer," says Sawday's Sarah Bolton

They arrived one hot afternoon in June, a trio of tiny piglets looking forlorn and not a little sunburnt. Three runts according to our pig guru, Nicola, "Look at them, they can barely walk, they're too thin and they won't last," she said cheerily. How wrong she was. A bed of straw, a spot of factor fifty on the ears, a tonne of food and they're as pinky and perky as anything.

More surprising than the piggies' recovery is the effect they've had on the Sawday's staff. We're mostly a bunch of townies whose experience of animal-rearing never went beyond owning a cat.

My boss Rob is just one of the urbanites who has had his head well and truly turned by the porkers. The sight of the little ones standing on their hind legs in anticipation of a few tasty morsels at lunchtime has done for him. Lately, I've heard him saying that he just happened to notice some short-date bread at the shop, and bought it as an extra treat for the two Berkshires and the three little pigs. He arrives each morning laden with fruit and veg. For all I know he's been up since 3.30am to catch the markets.

But that's the nice thing about having animals and a community farm next to the office: it brings out a bit of the country in the most hardened townies. Even I nip over the road, in my gold sandals, carefully dodging the beastly nettles, to marvel at all the veg and say hello to the pigs. I walk past what, six months ago, was an un-prepossessing piece of land that is now dazzling in its abundance: beans studded with scarlet shimmying up the old bamboo, vast squashes lurking under a shady canopy, and huge patches of potatoes and onions. The chooks are funny. They like spaghetti - Rob brings that in, too - I guess it's like worms. They gather in their run shaking their tail feathers and squawking - a real life hen-do.

I'm not entirely sure where the Slow bit comes in - it seems like hard work this farming lark. I see the growers nipping in a few times a day to feed the animals, clean out the chickens, thin the carrots, water and weed. I call lazing around on a lounger, or taking an extra hour to get ready with my husband waiting by the door, going 'slow'.

There has been talk of introducing some bees, oh, and a donkey. But donkeys get lonely, so maybe two donkeys. Oh lawks, this is how Noah's Ark, the local farm theme park, began and now they've got a giraffe and a couple of rhinos. I look forward to seeing my boss going out to feed the likes of them at lunchtime. For now we're happy leaving our desks, emails and cares behind for a bit and visiting the chooks and piglets. Uh-oh, I think I'm getting in touch with my inner farmer.

Go Slow series

Go Slow England

'Slow' embraces an appreciation of good food and artisan producers, of craftsmanship and community, landscape and history. In this guide we have a terrific selection of Special Places to Stay owners who offer a counter-balance to our culture of haste and take their time to enjoy life at its most enriching. You will discover an unusual emphasis on inspiring people and will meet farmers, literary people, wine-makers and craftsmen – all rich with stories to tell.

Praise for Go Slow England:

"If you need a break from the rat race, you'll find it here." **Waitrose Food Illustrated**

"If one book sums up what life is like outside England's cities, this is it. It's a homemade-cake-and-jam sort of a book." **Sunday Times Magazine**

"Discover rural idylls, country retreats and slow, slow living as you lie back, stretch out and enjoy the view." **The Guardian**

"This book is a real pleasure and a superb celebration of the best of English life."
The Good Book Guide

"Go Slow England is a magnificent guidebook." **BBC Good Food Magazine**

Go Slow Italy

We have handpicked forty-six exceptional places to stay in Italy – birthplace of the Slow movement, home of Slow Food. From the mountainous north, through cypress-dotted Tuscany and on down to the gutsy, colourful south, you will discover owners with an unmatched passion for Slow Food and Slow Travel. Meet farmers, literary people, wine-makers, olive oil producers and craftsmen – all with rich stories to tell. Go Slow Italy celebrates fascinating people, fine architecture, history, landscape and real food.

Praise for Go Slow Italy:

"One of my favourite books of the year."
Amanda Robinson, Editor Italia! Magazine

> **To order any of these books**
> Call 01275 395431 or visit our online bookshop www.sawdays.co.uk/bookshop for up to 40% discount

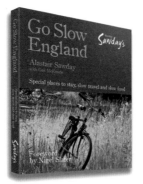

Go Slow England UK £19.99 Paperback

Go Slow Italy UK £19.99 Paperback

Go Slow France

Living the Slow life comes naturally to the French as they wander down to the boulangerie in the morning for freshly baked baguettes, buy veg, saucissons and bright-eyed fish from their local market or tuck into long and lazy lunches at a family-run restaurant. Let the slower pace of life rub off on you as you explore with Go Slow France.

The range of people and places is pretty amazing: from Alpine chalet to Pyrenean mountain refuge, goat farmers of the May '68 generation to landed gents in their utterly classic family château; a poet with yurts; a couple of sisters living quietly, organically, in the country and keeping up with all things international to feed the conversation with foreign guests at dinner; a Brit in Provence, whose bones have turned French through love of the place, people, food and wine; artists and historians, a collector of weighing scales, and one of the founders of an early gastropub who left swinging London with his designer wife to bring up a family in saner, healthier climes: the remotest part of central France.

We celebrate the eccentricities of these really special places to stay and the vivaciousness of their owners. Visit them and you will drink wine from their own vineyards and eat vegetables from their own potagers.

Eat Slow Britain

Eat Slow Britain celebrates forty-three of Britain's most special places to eat. You'll meet owners and chefs who grow their own food, source only the very best local produce, often direct from farmers, and who prepare it all with love and flair. Best of all, they have created beautiful spaces and convivial atmospheres and want to you come and enjoy it all at your leisure. Discover the flavours of British foods: menus lovingly composed from local larders, the freshest ingredients worked into something magical. Eat Devon Red Ruby beef, hand-dived Lyme Bay scallops, Highland venison, partridge fresh from the Lammermuirs, porcini, chanterelles and wood blewits from Ashdown forest.

Published in collaboration with the Soil Association, Eat Slow Britain also focuses on some of Britain's best organic food producers. You'll find artisan cheese makers, master bakers, farmers and brewers. Many have farm shops, cafés and teashops to visit too and each is working with minimal effect on the environment, safeguarding the countryside for future generations and protecting a sense of tradition and regionality.

Fresh writing and beautiful photography make this book a must for lovers of real food and for those who like to eat in restaurants where chefs have a strong sense of place.

Go Slow France UK £19.99 Paperback

Eat Slow Britain UK £19.99 Paperback

Slow Travel to our Special Places

Page	Property name	Nearest station	Free pick-up?
24	Primrose Valley Hotel	St Ives	Free
28	Cornish Tipi Holidays	Bodmin Parkway	No
32	Wooda Farm	Bude / bus from Exeter.	For a fee
36	Hornacott	Plymouth	No
40	Fingals	Totnes	For a charge
44	Agaric Rooms at Tudor House	Newton Abbot	No
48	Beara Farmhouse	Barnstaple	No
52	The Bull Hotel	Dorchester	By arrangement
56	North Wheddon Farm	Taunton	No
60	Royal Oak Inn	Taunton	No
64	Binham Grange	Blue Anchor	Free
68	Huntstile Organic Farm	Bridgwater	By arrangement
72	Church Cottage	Bridgwater	Free
76	Barwick Farm House	Yeovil Junction	Free
80	Harptree Court	Castle Cary	No
84	The Griffin Inn	Haywards Heath	No
88	Dadmans	Sittingbourne/Faversham	For a charge
100	1 Leicester Meadows	King's Lynn	No
104	Strattons	Downham Market	10% discount for no-car guests
108	24 Fox Hill	Crystal Palace	Free
112	The Victoria	Barnes	No
116	Abbey Home Farm	Kemble	No
120	Ty-Mynydd	Hereford	No
124	The Peren	Hereford	By arrangement
128	Little Quebb Cottages	Hereford	Yes
132	Old Country Farm	Colwall/Malvern	Free
136	Annie's Cabin	Ludlow	Free
140	Timberstone Bed & Breakfast	Ludlow	Free
144	Manor Farm	Cromford	No
156	Gallon House	Knaresborough	Free
160	Daffodil & Daisy	Penrith	For a fee
164	Southlands Farm	Hexham	Free by arrangement
168	Thistleyhaugh	Alnmouth/Morpeth	No
172	West Coates	Berwick-upon-Tweed	Free
184	Allt-y-bela	Newport	No
188	Court Farm	Abergavenny	Free
192	Gliffaes Hotel	Abergavenny	Free if staying 3+ nights
196	Penpont	Abergavenny	No
200	The Yat	Builth Wells	No
204	fforest	Carmarthen/Aberystwyth	No
208	The Kinmel Arms	Abergele-Pensarn	Free
212	Neuadd Lwyd	Bangor	No

www.sawdays.co.uk

You'll find the entire collection of over 5,000 Special Places on our website and can find out more about the places in this book, too, such as whether you need to book for dinner or pay for breakfast or whether you can take your child or your dog.

Place index